"With refreshing clar[...]
resurrection not only [...]
an excellent resource for personal devotions or a group Bible study."

David Hazzard currently serves as one of the
Executive Officers of the Pentecostal Assemblies of Canada,
has pastored in both Edmonton and Toronto, and taught
at Pan Africa Christian College in Nairobi.

"*Easter Unwrapped* is the powerful story of our faith walk. In eleven
short and succinct chapters, John Telman opens the story to each
reader. I hope that as you read this book, you will encounter the
central figure of the story. When you find Jesus, you find life!"

Dr. Fel Bagunu is the Lead Pastor at GracePointe
Community Church in Lee's Summit, Missouri,
which he and his wife Dianna planted. Fel has a
Doctorate from Fuller Theological Seminary.

"I highly recommend *Easter Unwrapped* to any layman or scholarly
Christian who wants to revisit the scriptures for a well-supported
view of what Easter is really all about. If you are looking for stories
about Bunny Rabbits and Easter Eggs, this is not for you. If you
want a good read that will make your day, then this is the book."

Gerald Onciul has been Assistant Principal French Horn
Chair with the Edmonton Symphony Orchestra since 1977.
He was Professor of Horn at the University
of Alberta from 1992 – 2008.

"In *Easter Unwrapped*, John paints a simple, yet profound picture of the reality and power of the Resurrection. I thoroughly enjoyed how he brought forth deep biblical truths using relatable illustrations and personal testimonies. This book reads very much like a Gospel narrative, which goes to show just how inspired, passionate, and convicted the author is over its message. I believe that when you read it, you will most certainly find yourself holding the same conviction."

Jason Silver is Lead Pastor of New Victory Church
in Calgary, Alberta, Canada.

"'He lives' is the most important message we can hear today because it is true. Jesus conquered death and is now with us always. Thank you, John, for this incredible look at the Resurrection. Everyone needs to read *Easter Unwrapped* and remove any doubt from their hearts about this eternity-changing miracle."

Joe Bonsall is tenor with the American music group
The Oak Ridge Boys, and author of ten books.

"John Telman reminds us of the powerful event that Easter represents. Coming from different angles of the Easter story, he brings the resurrection of Jesus back to the forefront of our faith where it belongs, skillfully unwrapping the story with scripture to bring his points home."

Joey Vazquez was a member of the
Brooklyn Tabernacle in Brooklyn, N.Y., for 30 years.
He is now the senior pastor of Deep Waters Tabernacle in
Maryland, which he planted with his wife Missy.

"What a great book—*Easter Unwrapped* touched my heart. I love how it balances an easy read with strong points to back up the discussion on the life-giving promise of the Resurrection! May this book touch your heart and mind by encouraging you to reach towards the true meaning of Easter."

> Dr. Lana Olsen is a faculty research associate at ASU Center for Sustainable Tourism.

"*Easter Unwrapped* uncovers the facts behind the often-misunderstood celebration which most know as Easter—of the Death and Resurrection of Christ Jesus. It is likely more significant than Christmas; the gift of his life for us."

> Mark Wicks is an evangelist and missionary to the Philippines.

"John Telman has created a remarkably comprehensive reminder of the true significance of Christ's resurrection in *Easter Unwrapped*! He takes readers on a journey, starting with the shock of awe when it was realized that Jesus was no longer in the tomb. He then goes on to highlight exactly why that was so significant! *Easter Unwrapped* is a timely and uplifting reminder that Jesus knows us, he loves us, and he serves us! Most of all, it reminds us that Jesus is not a past tense savior! He lives!"

> Mary Pulley is a television news personality and content strategist. She serves on the board of directors of the United Way of Wyandotte County Kansas.

"In a dark and dying world, the resurrection power of Jesus Christ is the only hope. It was through tear filled eyes that I read this book, captivated and encouraged by the scriptures and stories that John Telman shared. *Easter Unwrapped* is a powerful encouragement to believers, a powerful tool for those who are wavering in their faith, and an anointed witness to those who don't know Jesus and the power of his Resurrection! After reading this book, I can't imagine anyone ever doubting God's love for them."

Millie Gray is a Kansas City police officer,
and Sergeant in the United States Air Force.

"Let *Easter Unwrapped* be the message of the Resurrection. The way in which John tells this story will transform followers of Jesus Christ. Your thoughts and your emotions will be engaged, and your faith will be challenged as you journey into the deeper meaning of the Easter season. Prepare your heart for a richer, deeper understanding of the Resurrection."

Dr. Vickie Murillo is superintendent of
Council Bluffs Community School District.

"What fun it is to unwrap a gift. But the real joy is in the gift itself! In *Easter Unwrapped*, John Telman shows us the incredible gift we have received in the Resurrection of Jesus Christ. And it is definitely worth unwrapping! Easter is bigger than you think!"

Scott Wesley Brown is an
acclaimed contemporary Christian songwriter,
recording artist with 25 albums, and pastor of
Sonship Community Church in North County, San Diego.

Easter
UNWRAPPED

Easter
UNWRAPPED

11 INSIGHTS
INTO THE DEEPER
MEANING OF
THE SEASON

JOHN W. TELMAN

EASTER UNWRAPPED
Copyright © 2019 by John W. Telman

Printed in Canada

ISBN: 978-1-4866-1243-7

Word Alive Press
119 De Baets Street, Winnipeg, MB R2J 3R9
www.wordalivepress.ca

Cataloguing in Publication may be obtained through Library and Archives Canada

DEDICATION

To Jeremy Michael Telman, my son. This is for you. Jesus is your risen LORD and Savior, and he loves you even more than I could.

CONTENTS

Acknowledgements

This book is the result of input by numerous people that I want to acknowledge. Carole, my wife, has long been the first person I pass my writing through. She has a way of encouraging and challenging simultaneously. Her wisdom is quite remarkable. I've often said that she is the smart one in the family.

Many thanks to my good friend, Richard Piech, for reading the draft and making wonderful contributions. Rich, let's play some racquetball. I'll pay.

Word Alive Press has been a pleasure to work with, and I highly recommend them to all writers. Lastly, I would like to acknowledge my LORD and Savior, Jesus Christ, who gave me life and inspires me.

FOREWORD
Dr. Darrell SC Peregrym

As far back as I can remember, Christmas and Easter have been a significant part of my life every year. Growing up in a Christian family certainly affected the importance of these celebrations due to our belief and faith in Jesus Christ. However, as a child and young teen, what I remember most was the church events and family gatherings where I experienced so much love and joy. Words could not adequately describe the feeling, but my heart most definitely felt it.

After all these years, I still look forward to, and love, both Christmas and Easter. In my mind and heart there was always a common denominator that tied them together for me: Jesus Christ. As a youngster I was unable to identify or explain it, but as I got older I realized that it was my personal relationship with Jesus Christ that was the unifying factor. This was evident in our church and family gatherings as well. Jesus was and is the common denominator—the Divine link. Not only spiritually, but physically and emotionally.

John writes in his third book, *Christmas Unwrapped*, "At the very foundation of both holidays is the love of God for his creation."[1] This was truly the essence and foundation of my experience. The presence of God's love was what made our church events and gatherings around Christmas and Easter so genuine and palpable. Not because of a religious perspective, but because of a relational connection with God through Jesus Christ.

Christmas Unwrapped began the journey into a deeper understanding of the love of God for his creation (you and me) being extended through His Son, Jesus Christ. I believe John's sequel, *Easter Unwrapped*, completes the journey for us. In doing so, John brings us face-to-face with Almighty God, our Heavenly Father and Creator, who loves us and offers us a personal relationship with Him. John helps us to see and understand not only the "Jesus of Christmas," who is Emmanuel—*"God with us"* (Matthew 1:23, NIV)—but also the "Jesus of the Cross and Resurrection", who is our Lord and Savior (Luke 2:10-11).

Jesus openly declared his direct connection to His Father, who is God, our Heavenly Father. The Gospel of John 14:6-7 and 9-11 (NIV) records Jesus saying it in many different ways.

> I am the way, and the truth, and the life. No one comes to the Father except through me. If you really know me, you will know my Father as well. … Anyone who has seen me has seen the Father … Don't you believe that

---

1 John W. Telman, *Christmas Unwrapped* (Winnipeg: Word Alive Press, 2017), 2.

I am in the Father, and that the Father is in me? The
words I say to you I do not speak on my own authority.
Rather, it is the Father, living in me, who is doing His
work. Believe me when I say that I am in the Father and
the Father is in me; or at least believe on the evidence of
the works themselves.

In *Easter Unwrapped*, John methodically helps us to see Jesus
Christ through the miracles of the Cross and the Resurrection in
such a manner that we cannot help but come face-to-face with God
and His love for us. John's insights prompt us to view the events
around the Cross and Resurrection through a different lens, revealing the critical link between the two. Both were essential to our
forgiveness and redemption, thereby setting us free from the hold of
sin, death, judgment and Hell in our lives. John says it well in chapter three: "If the cross is the *payment* for our sins, the empty tomb
is the *receipt*, showing that the perfect Son of God made complete
payment for our sins."

Christmas is when we celebrate the Gift and Promise of Jesus Christ, and Easter is when we celebrate the fulfillment of the
promise through the Cross and Resurrection of Jesus Christ. It is
John 3:16 (NIV) being fulfilled: "For God so loved the world that
he gave his one and only Son, that whoever believes in him shall not
perish but have eternal life."

As you read through the following pages, I encourage you to
open your heart and mind to the insights John presents and consider
what they mean, or could mean, for you personally—for today and
all of eternity. As I read of the actions and words of Jesus, and the

events before, during and after the Cross and Resurrection, I found myself becoming more and more grateful and excited for who God is and His enduring love for me, and for all mankind.

The crucifixion of Jesus Christ on the cross, and His subsequent resurrection, are God the Father's love in action as He fulfills His promises. I am reminded of God's faithfulness, and His ongoing promises for me. I am also thankful for the promises that have been fulfilled, and so very excited for the fulfillments forthcoming. John writes of both as he presents the contrasting pictures of Jesus in Chapter 11.

Essentially, through these pages, John is calling us to see Easter in a fresh new light as we reconsider the Cross and Resurrection. John challenges us to know the God who did all this for us in order to show His love and desire to know us, and have a personal relationship with us.

For me, Easter is truly not about the chocolates or the bunnies; however, I am not offended by those who enjoy them. It is not an either/or situation for me. Enjoy the chocolate, pet the bunnies, but do not let that be your primary or only focus for Easter.

The primary focus is the love of God revealed through the Cross and Resurrection. We needed the Crucifixion in order for Jesus Christ to pay for our sins and redeem us, and we needed the Resurrection of Jesus for our salvation and new eternal life.

In chapter four, John writes, "The resurrection is the single most important event in human history. Without it there is no salvation, no hope of eternal life, no point to this existence." I would agree!

However it does not end there ... the second most important event in *your* human history is what you will choose to do with the truth of Easter. Will you choose to accept the love of Almighty God that our Heavenly Father is extending to you, and enter into a personal relationship with Him through the Jesus of Easter, our Lord and Savior?

I would encourage you to read through the pages of this book with an open mind and heart, and see if there is truly any good reason why you would not! For me, I could not find any good reason and I have never regretted my decision to accept God's offer of love through His Son, the Jesus Christ of Christmas and Easter. I pray that this will prove to be the case for you as well.

Dr. Darrell SC Peregrym has a multi-vocational global ministry as a pastor, professor, leadership coach and businessman. He serves as President of Integrity Etc Leadership and Heart of the Nations Ministries, and is an Adjunct Professor at Trinity Western University in BC, Canada, and George Fox University/Portland Seminary in Oregon, USA. He is also the President of ICCL Seminary in Kiev, Ukraine, and the Eusebia Rarama Foundation in the Philippines.

INTRODUCTION

My preference is to refer to Easter Sunday as Resurrection Sunday. Far from my mind are the trappings of bunny rabbits and chocolate eggs. This special day is a celebration of life. Nothing is more important to you and to me than Resurrection Sunday.

Life is more than a beating heart. It's more than what you taste, touch or see. You are more than a physical body. You're a living soul. The sad fact is that most people are dead on the inside. If you carefully read Paul's words to the Ephesians, zombies seem realistic.

> I also pray that you will understand the incredible greatness of God's power for us who believe him. This is the same mighty power that raised Christ from the dead and seated him in the place of honor at God's right hand in the heavenly realms. Now he is far above any ruler or authority or power or leader or anything else—not only in this world but also in the world to come. God has put all things under the authority of Christ and has made him head over all things for the benefit of the church. And the church is his body; it is made full and

complete by Christ, who fills all things everywhere with himself. Once you were dead because of your disobedience and your many sins.
—Ephesians 1:19-2:1, NLT

Those who have seen the movies *Night of the Living Dead*, *Zombieland* or *I Am Legend* have seen dead bodies moving about. The apostle Paul was accurate when he taught that even though there may be signs of physical life, death maybe on the inside.

The first prophecy given was given by God to the first man.

The Lord God placed the man in the Garden of Eden to tend and watch over it. But the Lord God warned him, "You may freely eat the fruit of every tree in the garden—except the tree of the knowledge of good and evil. If you eat its fruit, you are sure to die."
—Genesis 2:15-17, NLT

That day didn't see the physical death of Adam. Rather, Adam died on the inside. What's worse is that death was introduced to all of us. But why all this talk of death when Easter is about resurrection and life? Simply put, without the resurrection of Jesus, we would all be stuck in the thick slime of sin. We would have been limited to physical life and the prospect of eternal death once our bodies stopped. Remember, you are more than a body. Do words hurt? Do you feel with more than your physical senses? Of course, but this world treats you like you are nothing but a body to be manipulated, abused and used.

The resurrection is about life. It is God's way of showing us that death is a certainty but not a necessity. You don't need to be dead on the inside. You can live even when your body stops. Isn't it amazing that our eternity is our choice? The creation of who you are was *not* your choice, but whether you experience eternal life or not *is* your choice. Think about that for a moment.

As you read this book, I encourage you to think about what life truly is. It's so much more than merely physical pleasure, and it's even more than the seventy-odd years that the average person will physically live on this earth. The resurrection changed everything. It gave us meaning, purpose and quality, even if our physical life is less than perfect.

One of my favorite Greek words from the New Testament is *zoe*. In chapter 8, you will read more about this wonderful word that is contrasted with other Greek words that we translate "life." It is about more than physical existence. Possibly the most quoted and well-known verses from the Bible is John 3:16—and it includes the aforementioned word. In fact, you will read the word *zoe* often in the Gospel of John. Life is what God is all about. He is the creator and sustainer of life. His desire is that we experience a new life that resurrects us from death that sin caused.

> *God loved the world so much that he gave his one and only Son, so that everyone who believes in him will not perish but have eternal life (zoe).*
> —John 3:16, NLT

When "life" hits you between the eyes, when you feel the darkness of death around, when you're faced with trouble that drains the "life" out of you, remember Resurrection Sunday. It was the day that changed everything, and it's more than chocolate and bunny rabbits.

chapter one

THE START OF SOMETHING NEW

*On the first day of the week, at early dawn, they came to the tomb
bringing the spices which they had prepared. And they found the stone
rolled away from the tomb, but when they entered, they did not find the
body of the Lord Jesus. While they were perplexed about this, behold,
two men suddenly stood near them in dazzling clothing; and as the
women were terrified and bowed their faces to the ground, the men said
to them, "Why do you seek the living One among the dead? He is not
here, but He has risen. Remember how He spoke to you while He was
still in Galilee, saying that the Son of Man must be delivered into the
hands of sinful men, and be crucified, and the third day rise again."
And they remembered His words, and returned from the tomb and
reported all these things to the eleven and to all the rest.*

—Luke 24:1-9, NASB

Surprise! Surprise!

The women did not expect to experience what they
did on that amazing day. They came to the tomb, and found
two men standing by them in shining garments. Even as angels

announced the birth of Jesus (Luke 2:8-15), so they also announced his resurrection. The announcement of his birth was made to a few humble folks—those considered unimportant by the world. His resurrection was announced by angels to a few women who were also not considered important. They saw physically at first, but then they truly perceived.

It's great to have empirical evidence, but the confirmed prophecy given by Jesus is the greatest witness to the truth. Jesus told the disciples before the crucifixion that *"the Son of Man must suffer many things and be rejected by the elders and chief priests and scribes, and be killed and be raised up on the third day"* (Luke 9:22, NASB). The angels reminded them of what Jesus had said.

JESUS WAS DELIVERED INTO THE HANDS OF SINFUL MEN

It's dangerous to be delivered into the hands of sinful men, but that is what happened to Jesus Christ. The sinless, perfect Son of God was handed over to the wicked. Dangerous places and people are routinely avoided, but Jesus, the all-powerful, all-knowing Son of God was delivered into the hands of sinful men. John 10:39, Matthew 12:14, Mark 3:6 and Mark 11:18 tell us that evil men were devising a way to kill Jesus. But they could not accomplish their plan until the moment that God had planned.

The sad fact is that the "evil men" included the religious. Religion does not save anyone from sin, but relationship with Jesus Christ cleanses from all unrighteousness. He forgives! Jesus even forgave a criminal that was being crucified alongside him.

Many evil men have come and gone. Sennacherib, Hitler, Stalin, Mao Tse-tung, Idi Amin Dada, and Abu Musab Al-Zarqawi are just a few of the evil men that this world has seen, but David said, *"In God have I put my trust: I will not be afraid what man can do unto me"* (Psalms 56:11, KJV). These men and others brought fear to the lives of many, but Jesus Christ came and was delivered into the hands of evil men like them.

Jesus Was Crucified

The angels reminded the women that Jesus knew he was going to be killed. Jesus knew he was going to be crucified because he has all knowledge, but he also knew because scripture declared it.

The prophecy of Isaiah 53:8 says, *"he was cut off out of the land of the living: for the transgression of my people was he stricken"* (KJV). God loves all people so much that the punishment for sin was laid upon the perfect Son of God. God's love is not just for pretty or successful people, but for all!

How much does God love? Romans 5:8-9 (NASB) tells us that, *"God demonstrates His own love toward us, in that while we were yet sinners, Christ died for us. Much more then, having now been justified by His blood, we shall be saved from the wrath of God through Him."*

The crucifixion of Jesus, while horrible, was the ultimate sign of God's love for sinful and rebellious humanity. In a day where terrorists often literally crucify people, we are reminded that God permitted the crucifixion of Jesus. Beyond simply giving permission, it actually pleased God for something so horrible to take place. *"He had done no wrong and had never deceived anyone. But he was buried like*

3

a criminal; he was put in a rich man's grave. But it was the Lord's good plan to crush him and cause him grief. Yet when his life is made an offering for sin, he will have many descendants. He will enjoy a long life, and the Lord's good plan will prosper in his hands" (Isaiah 53:9-10, NLT). It might surprise you but God loves us that much. Jesus, the sinless Son of God, took the punishment and experienced death on the ultimate scale so that all could live eternally.

JESUS ROSE AGAIN

The angels also reminded the women that Jesus had said he would rise again. The Bible tells us that besides Jesus, seven individuals were raised from the dead. However, Christ's resurrection was unique in that all the others died again. Jesus is alive!

Jesus knew he would be raised from the grave. He told the Jews,

> *"Destroy this temple and in three days, I will raise it up." The Jews then said, "It took forty-six years to build this temple and will You raise it up in three days?" But He was speaking of the temple of His body. So, when He was raised from the dead, His disciples remembered that He said this; and they believed the Scripture and the word Jesus had spoken.*

—John 2:19-22, NASB

A few details about Jesus after he rose are important to us all.

- The risen Christ had a real human body that was recognizable (Luke 24; John 20:26-29).

4

- His body was composed of flesh and bones (Luke 24:39-40).
- His body could be handled and touched; therefore, it had to have substance (Matthew 28:9;
- John 20:27).
- His skin showed scars and nail prints; his body retains the scar of the wound in his side and hands (Luke 24:39).
- He breathed (John 20:22).
- He carried on conversations, so He had to have vocal cords and the use of air. His voice was immediately recognizable (Luke 24; John 20:16, 26).
- He ate, so His body had a digestive system (Luke 24:30).

More than three hundred verses in the New Testament are concerned with the subject of Jesus' resurrection. "But the ultimate proof of the resurrection for each individual lies in his own knowledge of the risen Christ, for in this matter the evidence of experience can supplement that of history"[2] writes J. Anderson, who was professor of Oriental Law and the director of the Institute for Advanced Legal Studies at the University of London.

At a crucial moment in history, people in England were anxiously awaiting news. Their only means of communication was a

---

2   J. Norman Anderson, *The Evidence for the Resurrection* (Downers Grove, IL: Intervarsity Press, 1950), 16.

system of signal lights flashed across the English Channel. The fog became so dense that only a part of the message was made out. It read, "Wellington defeated." Gloom settled upon the English. But imagine their joy when the fog lifted and they received the whole message, "Wellington defeated the enemy." When Jesus Christ was crucified, His disciples were so surrounded by the fogs of doubt that they saw but one meaning to the sad event, "Christ defeated." All hope was gone; Jesus was dead. But early that morning brought the glorious fact of the risen Lord, and the message read, "Christ defeated the devil." How glorious!

By dying, Jesus Christ conquered the grave; by ascending, Christ made possible our ascension even to heaven. Hallelujah! *"O death, where is thy sting? O grave, where is thy victory? ... Thanks be to God, which giveth us the victory through our Lord Jesus Christ"* (I Corinthians 15:55, 57, KJV).

The angels reminded the women of what Jesus said; we, too, are reminded of what Jesus said, and that what he said actually happened! Jesus Christ is the way, the truth and the life. We can trust what he said.

Today is the start of something new! Jesus said:

- "All things are possible with God" (Mark 10:27, NASB).
- "Do not worry about tomorrow" (Matthew 6:34, NASB).
- "Come to Me, all who are weary and heavy-laden, and I will give you rest" (Matthew 11:28, NASB).

- "In the world you have tribulation but take courage; I have overcome the world." (John 16:33, NASB).

Jesus said much more and great attention has been given to what he has said. Both now and when he walked the dusty road of Judea, his words have had a powerful effect on all. People argued about what he said, as they do even today, but what he said about his resurrection is infinitely more important than anything else because it gives us hope and courage in the face of death and eternal separation from our creator. In addition, the fact that Jesus rose, as he said he would, is proof that everything he said was true.

We can commit our lives to him on the basis of the resurrection. Today, this very day, is the start of something new because Jesus rose from the dead! Jesus also said, *"...God so loved the world, that He gave His only begotten Son, that whoever believes in Him shall not perish, but have eternal life. For God did not send the Son into the world to judge the world, but that the world might be saved through Him"* (John 3:16-17, NASB). Anyone who will accept Jesus as their Savior and commit their lives to him will experience the start of something new that will continue forever!

chapter two

THE END OF AGONY

God publicly endorsed Jesus the Nazarene by doing powerful miracles, wonders, and signs through him, as you well know. But God knew what would happen, and his prearranged plan was carried out when Jesus was betrayed. With the help of lawless Gentiles, you nailed him to a cross and killed him. But God released him from the horrors of death and raised him back to life, for death could not keep him in its grip. King David said this about him:

"I see that the Lord is always with me. I will not be shaken, for he is right beside me. No wonder my heart is glad, and my tongue shouts his praises! My body rests in hope. For you will not leave my soul among the dead or allow your Holy One to rot in the grave. You have shown me the way of life, and you will fill me with the joy of your presence."

Dear brothers, think about this! You can be sure that the patriarch David wasn't referring to himself, for he died and was buried, and his tomb is still here among us. But he was a prophet, and he knew God had promised with an oath that one of David's own descendants would sit on his throne. David was looking into the future and speaking of the Messiah's resurrection. He was saying that God would not leave him among the dead or allow his body to rot in the grave.

God raised Jesus from the dead, and we are all witnesses of this. Now he is exalted to the place of highest honour in heaven, at God's right hand. And the Father, as he had promised, gave him the Holy Spirit to pour out upon us, just as you see and hear today.

—Acts 2:22-33, NLT

Have you ever been disappointed when someone lets you down? You may have said something like, "I'll never trust anyone again." We all desire that medicine will work as a doctor says it should. We all expect a new car to run smoothly. When you sat on a chair this morning, you trusted that it would hold you up. Trusting is something we do many times every day of our lives. It will be a part of our lives forever.

For more than 36 years, Don Gorske of Fon Du Lac, Wisconsin, has eaten a Big Mac for lunch—every day; over 23,000 in total. He doesn't miss a lunch. He's predictable. Where do you think he'll be today at about noon? You guessed it—at McDonald's! Don is dependable. You can trust that he will be eating a Big Mac today.

In 1916, Pastor Thomas Chisholm was relieved of his pastoral duties by his church for having asthma and not preaching loudly enough. At fifty years old, He began travelling door to door on the dirt roads of Kentucky, selling brushes for a living. When most would have become discouraged, complained, or even quit, Thomas Chisholm did not. He praised God and pressed on. Seven years later, he penned a poem that we sing even now: "Great is Thy Faithfulness."

God is dependable! God is trustworthy. He keeps his promises! He had a plan to save humanity from destruction, and he accomplished it when he raised Jesus from the dead. The sacrifice of Jesus on the cross is the greatest sign of the love of God, but the raising of Jesus from the dead is the greatest sign of God's power.

There's a book titled *Days That Changed the World*.[3] It looks at the top fifty defining events that changed history. The book ends with the destruction of the Twins Towers of New York in September 2001. In this book, the death of Jesus Christ is mentioned, but there is no mention of his resurrection. It should be included, because there would be no hope at all if not for the resurrection of Jesus Christ. There would be complete despair if Jesus had not been raised from the dead.

How can we be sure that God has accepted the payment of the blood of Jesus? How do you know beyond a shadow of a doubt that you have been forgiven by God? The resurrection!

In Peter's sermon (found in Acts 2) we are reminded that God, who is dependable, does not give up, that he shows us the way of life, and that he gives us the joy of His presence.

GOD DOES NOT GIVE UP

Peter quotes Psalm 16 when he says that God does not abandon. God does not give up and if there was anyone who would have reason

---

3   Hywel Williams, *Days that Changed the World: The 50 Defining Events of World History* (Quercus, 2011).

to give up on mankind, it is God. We have no right to give up on anyone because we ourselves mess up and struggle with temptation.

God does not give up when we ignore him and turn to our own wicked ways. He continues to work remarkably in our lives, with loving patience and kindness. His desire is to give us real life and to keep us from destroying our own lives.

Notice Acts 2:25 (NASB): *"I saw the Lord always in my presence: for He is at my right hand so that I will not be shaken."* God is present so that he can steady us when the troubles of life come. The disciples were afraid and confused when Jesus died, but after the resurrection, Jesus said to them, *"Why are you troubled, and why do doubts arise in your hearts?"* (Luke 24:38, ESV). Jesus explained that it was necessary for him to suffer just as the scriptures had foretold, but God does not do things halfway. We are so grateful for the sacrifice of Jesus on the cross, but that is only part of the plan. He rose! God did not give up on us so Jesus Christ was raised, putting an end to the agony of death!

On that day, Peter arrived and went inside. Like the women who had first come on the scene, he also noticed the linen wrappings lying there, while the cloth that had covered Jesus' head was folded up and lying apart from the other wrappings. *"Then the disciple who had reached the tomb first also went in, and he saw and believed"* (John 20:8, NLT). The Greek word for Peter "noticing" (verse 6) is *theoreo*, which means he was theorizing or trying to understand. John entered the empty tomb after Peter, but the word used for him seeing (verse 8) is *horeo*. This subtle difference indicates that John did more than see with his eyes and try to figure the situation out. He clearly discerned what had happened. Peter may have been a bit slow, but

God did not give up on him. This is seen in the fact that it was Peter who preached to others about the risen Christ.

GOD SHOWS THE WAY OF LIFE

Peter reminds us that God doesn't give up on anyone and that he shows us the way of life. Jesus personalized what life is when he said, *"I am the resurrection and the life; he who believes in Me will live even if he dies, and everyone who lives and believes in Me will never die"* (John 11:25-26, NASB).

When Jesus Christ was raised from the dead, it was like no other miracle. As stated earlier, others who were brought back to life, like Lazarus and Jarius's daughter, eventually died, but Jesus is still alive and is in the throne room of God.

A Muslim in Africa became a Christian and some of his friends asked him why. He answered: "Suppose you were going down a road and suddenly the road forked in two directions. And you didn't know which way to go. If you met two men at the fork—one dead and one alive—which one would you ask to show you the way?" Obviously, you would follow the one who is living since he would be the only one to speak to you. Even now, God is speaking to your heart.

Jesus is truly alive and leads countless people to the way of life. Do you believe?

Believing means committing your trust to him when the flesh says, protect and serve yourself. To believe is more than just a mental recognition of Jesus: it's giving yourself 100% to him because he is the resurrection and the life.

Beyond temporary physical life, Jesus *is* the life and the one who gives us life. The angels said, *"Why do you seek the living One among the dead?"* (Luke 24:5, NASB).

Dr. J. Anderson wrote that Jesus "was unique in all He did; in all He said; in all He was. Whichever way one looks at Him, He is in a class by Himself. Even apart from the resurrection, there are excellent and convincing reasons for believing that He was 'God manifest in the flesh.' Is it, then, so incredible that such a One should rise from the dead? It would have been far more incredible if He had not."[4]

Jesus Christ shows us the way of life in his example. The apostle Paul wrote that Jesus was humble (Philippians 2) and Paul wrote that we too must have the same attitude. His way is love and reconciliation. Can you say that the love of God has changed you? Because Jesus was raised to life, we have a future. He made a way for us through his sacrifice and now that he has been raised, anyone who will commit their lives to him receives eternal life. It's his way. It's the way of life!

God does not give up on us. No matter how many times we self-destruct, he is right there to pick us up and forgive us if we will only give our lives fully to him. God shows us the way through the Son, Jesus Christ. He directs us how to live, and by his blood our sins are washed away. A bonus is that because Jesus rose we can experience joy!

---

4   Anderson, *The Evidence for the Resurrection*, 16.

GOD GIVES JOY (HIS PRESENCE)

The word that is used in verse 28 is *ufrasuna*. We get the English word "euphoria" from this Greek root. It's an intense feeling of "well-being" and "happiness." Since Jesus rose we can know the joy of God's presence.

I'll never forget the *ufrasuna* that I felt one day in Kansas City. I was playing the piano in church and felt the presence of God. It was so wonderful that I jumped up from the piano and ran the aisles of the church knocking over a plant on the way. To some it may have looked like I was a crazy man, but it was the joy of God's presence! There is no greater joy than knowing his presence because he is risen!

In his first letter, Peter wrote,

Blessed be the God and Father of our Lord Jesus Christ, who according to His great mercy has caused us to be born again to a living hope through the resurrection of Jesus Christ from the dead, to obtain an inheritance which is imperishable and undefiled and will not fade away, reserved in heaven for you, who are protected by the power of God through faith for a salvation ready to be revealed in the last time. In this you greatly rejoice, even though now for a little while, if necessary, you have been distressed by various trials, so that the proof of your faith, being more precious than gold which is perishable, even though tested by fire, may be found to result in praise and glory and honor at the revelation of Jesus Christ; and though you have not seen Him, you love Him, and though you do not see Him now, but believe

in Him, you greatly rejoice with joy inexpressible and full of glory,
obtaining as the outcome of your faith the salvation of your souls.
—I Peter I:3-9, NASB

The presence of the Lord is more than a comfort when you experience the troubles of life. His presence brings amazing joy right in the middle of fiery trials because Jesus is risen! Peter said that Jesus did not remain in the grave and that he and many others were witnesses to the fact of the resurrection. God was not willing for anyone to perish, so the Son of God left his throne and took on flesh, loved humanity and gave his life as payment for our salvation. He rose from the dead.

Three results of the resurrection that we learn from in Acts 2 are ...

1. My Heart is Glad
2. My Tongue Shouts His Praises
3. My Body Rests in Hope

The apostle Paul told the Christians in Rome, *"If the Spirit of Him who raised Jesus from the dead dwells in you, He who raised Christ Jesus from the dead will also give life to your mortal bodies through His Spirit who dwells in you"* (Romans 8:11, NASB). God is dependable! When Jesus said, "God so loved the world," it was proven by the Resurrection of Jesus Christ.

Have you ever told somebody you were sorry and they didn't accept your apology, as if it had made no difference? When Jesus was crucified and raised, God received us as if we had never sinned.

Those who will commit their very lives to God in faith receive the greatest gift of all—eternal life found in the very presence of the creator. Peter preached, *"God raised Him up again, putting an end to the agony of death"* (Acts 2:24, NASB). Eternity separated from the creator is and will be agony for those who turn away from the free gift of life in Jesus, but like Peter, we proclaim the death and resurrection of Jesus Christ.

chapter three

OF FIRST IMPORTANCE

I delivered to you as of first importance what I also received, that Christ died for our sins according to the Scriptures, and that He was buried, and that He was raised on the third day according to the Scriptures, and that He appeared to Cephas, then to the twelve. After that He appeared to more than five hundred brethren at one time, most of whom remain until now, but some have fallen asleep; then He appeared to James, then to all the apostles; and last of all, as to one untimely born, He appeared to me also.

—I Corinthians 15:3-8, NASB

We make decisions of importance every day. Do I start my diet today or next week? Do I say I love you now or later? Do I make a bank deposit today or tomorrow? Should I pray and read the Bible or watch TV? Should I sleep for another thirty minutes or get up now?

Paul told the Corinthian church what was "of first importance." Notice that the apostle Paul received the gospel from Jesus himself. He didn't get a hand-me-down gospel. He was only sharing what God told him. The great English preacher of the 19th century, Charles Spurgeon, once said, "We are not makers and inventors; we are repeaters, we tell the message we have received."[5] So let's look at what Paul said was "of first importance."

HE DIED FOR OUR SINS

Jesus Christ died—of that there is no argument.

- His enemies knew it. *". . .coming to Jesus, when they saw that He was already dead, they did not break His legs."* (John 19:33, NASB)
- His disciples knew it. *"She [Mary Magdalene] went and reported to those who had been with Him, while they were mourning and weeping. When they heard that He was alive and had been seen by her, they refused to believe it. After that, He appeared in a different form to two of them while they were walking along on their way to the country. They went away and reported it to the others, but they did not believe them either."* (Mark 16:10-13, NASB)

In fact, Luke 24:11 says that the disciples didn't believe that he was alive and that what was said seemed to them like "nonsense" (NASB).

---

5   C. H. Spurgeon, *The Complete Works of C. H. Spurgeon, Vol. 38* (Harrington: Delmarva, 2015).

Paul wrote that *"Christ died for our sins according to the scriptures"* (I Corinthians 15:3, NASB), as foretold in Isaiah 53.

Not only was his first-coming prophesied, his death for our sins was also prophesied (see Genesis 3:15; Isaiah 53:8; Psalm 22:15; Zechariah 12:10). God's plan was that the only one who could atone for our sins would die for them, and that was Jesus Christ, the sinless Son of God.

Many good people have died for others. My father was born and raised in Holland. It was the Canadians that came and liberated the Dutch from the Nazis. Many gave their lives and we are very grateful for their sacrifice, but it didn't cleanse anyone of sin. Those who died to liberate Holland did not die for the sins of the Dutch, but in contrast, Jesus died for our sins. Those who died in World War 2 did not want to die, but Jesus gave his life that the world might be saved from the destruction that is a result of sin (John 3:17). He was not a mere martyr, but gave himself up willingly and voluntarily (John 10:17; Gal. 2:20), in accordance with the purpose of God (Acts 2:23), as the Redeemer of the world.

Death is a horrible foe. Ezekiel 18:20 tells us that *"the soul who sins shall die"* (ESV). Not only the body dies; the soul does too. Everyone has to face this fact because all have sinned—except Jesus Christ. He was the only one who could put an end to death by offering himself as a sacrifice on behalf of all. He was the perfect sacrifice who died for my sins and yours.

HE WAS BURIED

Paul also reminded the Corinthians that Jesus Christ was buried. Living people are not buried.

Jesus was dead and was buried in a tomb. This was such a horribly powerful statement to those who loved him. Despair marked his disciples. In the ancient world, they would prepare dead bodies for burial by wrapping them in strips of cloth and a mixture of spices. Nicodemus, to whom Jesus spoke one night, came with about one hundred pounds of spices (John 19:40) to the tomb. The spices and aloes were poured into the folds of the strips of cloth, creating a cocoon-like sleeve.

As Joseph and Nicodemus prepared his body for burial, they saw the wounds, they saw the bruises and dried blood, and they knew he was dead. So they did what anyone would do for someone they loved—they buried him.

It is noteworthy that it was Nicodemus, a Pharisee, to whom Jesus spoke about life and salvation. In John 3, we read of their conversation. Jesus told Nicodemus, *"God so loved the world, that He gave His only begotten Son, that whoever believes in Him shall not perish, but have eternal life"* (John 3:16, NASB). This impacted Nicodemus. And later in John 7:50-52 we read that he came to the defence of Jesus and later, Nicodemus and Joseph were standing over a lifeless body.

The fact that Jesus died and was buried is of first importance because it is proof that he is not just a story, a ghost, a thought, an idea or an energy force, as New Age false teachers like to propose. He is 100% man and 100% God. He came, he suffered, he died and he was buried, but wait …

HE WAS RAISED

- on the third day
- according to the scriptures

These phrases show that it was God's plan all along. It was specific, historical and not just a fairy tale. Billy Graham once told *Time* magazine, "If I were an enemy of Christianity, I would aim right at the Resurrection, because that is the heart of Christianity."[6]

Lee Strobel, in his book *The Case for the Real Jesus*, outlines the attack on the resurrection of Jesus by atheists, Muslims, and Hindus. This title, part of a reading list with numerous volumes, is provided later in this book to help educate you, because the resurrection is the most important historical event.

The truth of history is that Jesus Christ died for our sins, was buried, and was raised. If the cross is the *payment* for our sins, the empty tomb is the *receipt*, showing that the perfect Son of God made complete payment for our sins. The payment itself is little good without the receipt! So much can be said about the resurrection of Jesus Christ, but consider the significance to you, me and every human that has ever lived.

Until 1981, Lee Strobel was a skeptic. Then something happened to Lee. He believed and the truth of the resurrection impacted him so much that he wrote two books that should be read by

---

6 Nancy Gibbs, The Message of Miracles, *Time Magazine* (June 24, 2001), http://content.time.com/time/magazine/article/0,9171,133993,00.html

everyone. *The Case for Christ* and *The Case for Faith* are analytical books that encourage those who believe and challenge those who don't.

Lee writes of Jesus . . .

He rose personally.
It was Jesus himself, not some substitute.

He rose bodily.
It was his crucified body that was raised from the dead.

He rose physically.
He wasn't a ghost or a phantom or a figment of someone's imagination.[7]

To say that he literally rose means that it really happened. Why does this matter? It matters since the Bible teaches that it is a fact. Paul said that it is "of first importance." Everything in the gospel records, everything in the book of Acts, everything in the epistles (pastoral letters) stands in perfect harmony on this point: Jesus died, was buried, and then rose from the dead.

Paul wrote to members of the Corinthian church, who were battling with Gnostic heresy. The Gnostic belief was and is that salvation comes not by Jesus' suffering, death and resurrection, but by his life of teaching and his establishing of the mysteries of his

---

7   Lee Strobel, *The Case for Christ: A Journalist's Personal Investigation of the Evidence for Jesus* (Grand Rapids: Zondervan, 2013).

work of salvation. Paul told the Corinthians that Jesus Christ died, was buried, was raised—and that he appeared.

HE APPEARED

Paul used the Greek word optanomai for "appeared," from which our English word "optic" was derived. It literally means "to see with the eyes" in contrast to seeing with the mind (in other words, understanding or perception).

In I Corinthians 15 (NASB), Paul says that...

1. *"He appeared to Cephas [Aramaic for Peter]"* (verse 5). After Pentecost, Peter preached a sermon on a street in Jerusalem and said, *"This Jesus God raised up again, to which we are all witnesses"* (Acts 2:32, NASB). Jesus appeared to the same man who denied he knew him! This is beautiful. It shows that God does not give up on anyone. He loves and reaches out to even those who turn their back on him.

2. *"He appeared ... to the twelve"* (verse 5). At this point, Judas had committed suicide and Thomas was missing, but Paul uses the title of "the twelve" to represent the men that Jesus had called to be his disciples. These were the men that he had spent much time with. These were the men whom he taught and gave the gospel. These were the men that were going to carry the gospel to the lost of Israel and the world.

He later appeared to Thomas, who eventually went to India and gave his life for the gospel.

3. *"He appeared to more than five hundred"* (verse 6). This again is a wonderful sign that God does not hide the joys of salvation. Gnostic teaching was that the mysteries were only for a select few, but Jesus appeared to hundreds of people at one time.

4. *"He appeared to James"* (verse 7). God's love is so amazing. James was one of the half-brothers of Jesus, and since his name always appears in scripture first, it is understood that he was the eldest of them. During his three years of ministry, we are told that "not even His brothers were believing in Him" (John 7:5, NASB). But he appeared to James, who later became a leader in the Jerusalem church. James testified to who Jesus Christ is, and it brought about his death by stoning in AD 62.

5. *"He appeared ... to all the apostles"* (verse 7). There were more than twelve apostles. Many are called apostle in the New Testament, but the Bible also cautions against people calling themselves an apostle if they have not been called by Jesus Christ. An apostle is someone that God sends as a representative or a missionary. In his letter to the Ephesians (4:11-13, NASB), Paul said, *"He (Jesus) gave some as apostles, and some as prophets, and some as evangelists, and some as pastors and teachers, for the equipping of the saints for the work of service, to the building up of the body of Christ; until we all attain to the unity of the faith,*

and of the knowledge of the Son of God, to a mature man, to the
measure of the stature which belongs to the fullness of Christ."
Jesus appeared to these who were sent.

6. "He appeared to Me" (verse 8). Paul met the risen Christ
   in a most memorable way. He was on his way to Da-
   mascus, Syria, to find, arrest, detain and possibly have
   Christians killed. Paul didn't know Jesus Christ, but
   Acts 9 tells of his encounter with Jesus. Even though
   Luke doesn't give us the details, Paul says that Jesus
   Christ appeared to him.

After he rose, Jesus himself said, "Do not be afraid; go and take
word to My brethren to leave for Galilee, and there they will see Me" (Matthew
28:10, NASB). Jesus Christ died, was buried, was raised on the third
day, and appeared to Peter, to the twelve, to five hundred, to James
and to Paul himself.

There are many important things in this life. Eating healthy,
drinking clean water, and getting plenty of sleep are foundational
to the physical needs of every human being. Peace of mind, love
and safety are also important. In addition to these things, we are
confronted with the reality of who Jesus Christ is. Paul said that "of
first importance" is the truth of the death, burial, resurrection and
appearance of Jesus Christ. He goes on to say, ". . .since by a man came
death, by a man also came the resurrection of the dead. For as in Adam all die, so
also in Christ all will be made alive" (1 Corinthians 15:21- 22, NASB).

In his letter to the Roman Christians, Paul wrote, "If you openly
declare that Jesus is Lord and believe in your heart that God raised him from the dead,
you will be saved" (Romans 10:9, NLT). To all who make the decision

to believe in who Jesus Christ is, Paul says, *"thanks be to God, who gives us the victory through our Lord Jesus Christ"* (I Corinthians 15:57, NASB).

There may seem to be many things in our lives that are important, but the death and resurrection of Jesus is "of first importance" to you, me and all of humanity.

chapter four

NOT HERE

After the Sabbath, as it began to dawn toward the first day of the week, Mary Magdalene and the other Mary came to look at the grave. And behold, a severe earthquake had occurred, for an angel of the Lord descended from heaven and came and rolled away the stone and sat upon it. And his appearance was like lightning, and his clothing as white as snow. The guards shook for fear of him and became like dead men. The angel said to the women, "Do not be afraid; for I know that you are looking for Jesus who has been crucified. He is not here, for He has risen, just as He said. Come, see the place where He was lying. Go quickly and tell His disciples that He has risen from the dead; and behold, He is going ahead of you into Galilee, there you will see Him; behold, I have told you."

And they left the tomb quickly with fear and great joy and ran to report it to His disciples. And behold, Jesus met them and greeted them. And they came up and took hold of His feet and worshipped Him. Then Jesus said to them, "Do not be afraid; go and take word to My brethren to leave for Galilee, and there they will see Me."

—Matthew 28:1-10, NASB

Have you ever lost your keys? I did. Two sets of keys were always in my pocket. One was for personal locks like home and car, and a second set was for the many locks at church. On a day that I won't easily forget, I drove to the church office only to notice that the church keys were not in my jacket pocket. I told my secretary that I was going home to look for them since they were important, so I turned around and drove another 30 minutes to my house. After searching for what felt like an hour, I could not find them. Do you wonder what I did? Well, I turned around and commuted back to the church to look for my keys. A custodian let me into my office but they weren't there. By now a couple of hours had passed, and my frustration began to build. Irritated, once again I drove home. After searching and finding no keys I sat down at my desk and thought I would write a note for Carole, my wife. I opened the drawer only to find, you guessed it, my keys. Half a day wasted. Have you ever lost your keys? I sure hope it didn't cost you a tank of gas and half a day of work.

When you expect your keys to be in one place and they aren't, your task is to go back and try to remember where they were last. On Resurrection Sunday, more than 2000 years ago, people were expecting to find the body of Jesus in the tomb but they heard the words, *"He is not here, for He has risen just as He said"* (Matthew 28:6, NASB).

On Resurrection Sunday, we celebrate the greatest event in human history. Greater than Wayne Gretzky scoring the most goals in NHL history; greater than winning an Oscar; greater than the completion of the Taj Mahal; greater than any other event in human history was the resurrection of Jesus.

If Christmas is a hollow holiday, it could be because the resurrection isn't important enough. In *Christmas Unwrapped*, I wrote, "When we think of Christmas and Easter, we may think of Santa Claus and the Easter Bunny. However, the truth is that these two characters do not represent the real meaning and intent of Christmas and Easter. At the very foundation of both Christmas and Easter is the love of God for his creation."[8]

The resurrection is the single most important event in human history. Without it there is no salvation, no hope of eternal life, no point to this existence. When you put this book down, please read I Corinthians 15. In this chapter, Paul emphasizes just how important the resurrection is.

JESUS SAID HE WOULD RISE

An angel told two women who were mourning the death of Jesus that he was not there.

They were expecting to find the body of Jesus but were reminded that Jesus said He would rise from the dead. *"Jesus began to show His disciples that He must go to Jerusalem, and suffer many things from the elders and chief priests and scribes, and be killed, and be raised up on the third day"* (Matthew 16:21, NASB).

It's amazing how dull our minds can become, and it's also amazing how God keeps his Word.

---

8   Telman, *Christmas Unwrapped*, 6.

The resurrection of Jesus guarantees salvation and life if you will only accept it. Whether or not you believe the chair in the corner will hold you, the chair is useless unless you sit on it. You must commit yourself. Unless we trust the words of Jesus that he would do what he said, we won't experience salvation and new life. Jesus said he would suffer, die and rise from the dead! Can you trust what Jesus said? We have a choice to either accept what he says or to believe he was a liar. There's no middle ground. It's interesting to note that eyewitnesses accepted his words as truth.

Jesus said many things that were very different from what others said. In fact, what he said put him on a collision course with a group of thinkers called Pharisees, as well as with others who had a following in the first century.

In Matthew 5, six times Jesus said, "You have heard, but I say unto you." Jesus spoke life, healing and restoration. Law looks to judge: "Who is guilty?" But Jesus spoke words of life. In agony on the cross, he spoke life to a thief who simply believed. Jesus said he would rise from the dead, destroying its hold on mankind. Anyone who will believe experiences new life.

JESUS MEETS WITH HIS DISCIPLES

Do you go to visit the grave of a loved one? My dear grandfather is buried in Edmonton.

He must be one of the greatest men who ever lived. He didn't invent anything. He never wrote a book or accomplished a great feat, but he was an amazing man because he knew and loved his Savior Jesus Christ. John Harold Huckle sang songs in church like,

"I would like to tell you what I think of Jesus," and he would tell you about his Lord but not without tears. He knew his God, and he lived his life daily with him. He endured much trouble in this life with such grace, beauty and love, all of which proved that Jesus Christ was with him. I had the honor of preaching his funeral and I know where his grave is—but the tomb of Jesus is empty!

The angel told the women that Jesus was not there but that he would meet with the disciples in Galilee, and sure enough, he did. He's unmistakable. There is no one like Jesus Christ. When you meet, him you know without a shadow of a doubt that he is who he said he was. Being good Jews, the disciples would not worship a mere man, but they knew who was standing before them (Matthew 28:17). Nothing shows others the sincerity of your beliefs more than your willingness to suffer and sacrifice for it. And the disciples suffered for their testimony that Jesus had risen from the dead. The disciples had no reason to go back to the tomb, because death had been defeated. "Look, he's not here." So, for those who will commit their lives to him, he will meet you where you are because he is risen!

Philip, born with Down syndrome, attended a third grade Sunday school class with several other eight-year-old boys and girls. The children did not readily accept Philip with all his differences, and often made fun of him. One Sunday the teacher brought L'Eggs pantyhose containers. They are the kind that look like large eggs. You may remember those L'Eggs containers if you lived in the 1970s. Each child was instructed to go outside on that lovely spring day and find a symbol of new life, and put it in the egg-like container. After running around on the church's property in wild confusion, the students returned to the classroom and placed their containers on the table. Surrounded by the children, the teacher began opening them one by one. After each one, whether a flower, a butterfly, a leaf, the class would "ooh" and "ahhhhh." Then one was opened, revealing nothing inside. The children exclaimed, "That's stupid! That's not fair! Somebody didn't do their assignment!" Then Philip spoke up, saying, "That's mine!" The children turned on him, saying, "Oh, Philip, you never do things right! There's nothing there. It's empty." Philip said, "The tomb was empty." Silence followed.

From then on, Philip became a fully accepted member of the class. He died not long afterward from an infection that most children would have shrugged off. At the funeral, this class of eight-year-olds marched up to the front, not with flowers, but together with their Sunday school teacher, each one of them laying in the casket an empty pantyhose egg.

Today's disciples of Jesus know him and know the truth that the tomb is empty, because they've met him.

JESUS SPEAKS LIFE

The words of Jesus always bring life and restoration. Jesus had good news for the women to tell, and we too have good news. Don't be afraid! Jesus Christ, the LORD and Savior lives!

Isn't it interesting that these ladies were doing as the angel told them? They were on their way to tell the disciples that Jesus was risen, so why did Jesus appear to them and tell them to do what they were already doing? Simply because of that one word: fear. Even though they were going, they were still afraid, and now for the second time, they were told not to fear! Friend, do not fear—Jesus is risen!

The Greek word for "fear" in verses 5 and 10 of Matthew 28 is *phobeo,* from which we get our English word "phobia."

The answer to whatever is troubling you is not fear, it's Jesus! Jesus speaks life to everyone, so we don't just encourage good morals. We tell people about the risen Christ who gives life!

Jesus told people not to be afraid! Read Matthew 14:27, 17:7, 28:10; Mark 5:36, 6:50; Luke 8:50, 12:4, 12:32; John 6:20; and Revelation 1:17. There is good reason not to be afraid! We do not fear anything because of who Jesus is! If you depend on your own cleverness or strength there is much reason to fear, but if you entrust your life to the hands of Jesus you do not have to fear! Fear is your choice, but why fear when Jesus Christ the Savior lives?

Jesus spoke life to the sick, he spoke life to the fearful, he spoke life to the hurt, and he spoke life to the broken! Fear will only choke life. Friend, don't be afraid! Jesus Christ is the risen Savior!

The implications of the resurrection are huge! If the resurrection did happen, then it proves:

- Jesus has power over death.
- You can personally trust him with your eternal destiny. Because he predicted and fulfilled his own resurrection, you can trust the promise he made to you about his intention to raise you from the dead.
- You can commit your very life to God.
- All other religions are false.

We've all heard someone say, "It doesn't matter what you believe so long as you are sincere." But that's not true. I can be sincere and still be wrong. I can sincerely believe that the airplane I am flying in will land just fine. But if the wheel falls off during landing, no amount of sincerity will prevent the plane from crashing. It's the same thing with our belief in Jesus. Either he rose from the dead or he did not. Sincerity is irrelevant. We are in debt to God because of our sin. We deserved death and judgment but the cross was the payment and the resurrection the receipt, proving that the payment was fully accepted. When anyone pounces on you when you make a mistake, point them back to the resurrection of Jesus and place your trust in God.

Carole and I keep our receipts and record how much we spend each month. Having a receipt is important when someone doubts payment was made. So, when someone doubts that you are forgiven and cleansed by the blood of Jesus, show them the receipt! The resurrection is that receipt. The cross is only part of the answer to life: the resurrection is the completion of the answer, and the empty tomb is the physical evidence.

chapter five

HEARTS AND MINDS

He Himself stood in their midst and said to them, "Peace be to you."
But they were startled and frightened and thought that they were seeing
a spirit. And He said to them, "Why are you troubled, and why do
doubts arise in your hearts? See My hands and My feet, that it is I
Myself; touch Me and see, for a spirit does not have flesh and bones
as you see that I have." And when He had said this, He showed them
His hands and His feet. While they still could not believe it because of
their joy and amazement, He said to them, "Have you anything here
to eat?" They gave Him a piece of a broiled fish; and He took it and
ate it before them.

Now He said to them, "These are My words which I spoke to you
while I was still with you, that all things which are written about Me
in the Law of Moses and the Prophets and the Psalms must be fulfilled."
Then He opened their minds to understand the Scriptures, and He said
to them, "Thus it is written, that the Christ would suffer and rise again
from the dead the third day, and that repentance for forgiveness of sins
would be proclaimed in His name to all the nations, beginning from
Jerusalem. You are witnesses of these things. And behold, I am sending

forth the promise of My Father upon you; but you are to stay in the city
until you are clothed with power from on high."
—Luke 24:36-49, NASB

God is all about life. Being the one and only creator, he is passionate about the life of his creation. The best proof of the existence of God is that there is life at all. The word "life" is found over five hundred times in the Bible. God is into life! Jesus said, "Truly, truly, I say to you, he who hears My word, and believes Him who sent Me, has eternal life, and does not come into judgment, but has passed out of death into life" (John 5:24, NASB).

> God is into life!
> There once was a very cautious man,
> who never laughed or cried.
> He never cared, he never dared.
> He never dreamed or tried.
> And when one day he passed away,
> his insurance was denied.
> For since he never really lived,
> they claimed he never died.[9]

God is into life! After being raised from the dead, Jesus appealed to the hearts and minds of his followers. You see, terrorism had taken place. Their leader had been brutally murdered, and they may have

---

9   Author unknown

been scared, anxious and worried that they would be next. Not only were their hearts troubled, but their minds were now doubting that Jesus was truly the Christ, the Son of the living God. But remember, God is into life! He proved it when he raised Jesus from the dead but to help us understand better, Jesus focused on hearts and minds.

HEARTS

"Peace be to you." Peace is a heart issue. Peace is not the lack of turmoil, but a posture right in the middle of trouble. Jesus asked a question that we need to be reminded of even today: *"Why are you troubled, and why do doubts arise in your hearts?"* (Luke 24:38, NASB). Jesus used the word *kardia*, from which we get our medical word "cardiac." The heart is the seat of our will and character. It's more than a physical organ, but understand that the physical organ can fail because of worry, fear, dread and anxiousness. *"Why are you troubled, and why do doubts arise in your hearts?"*

In a prophecy of what would happen, Jesus referred to *"Men's hearts failing them for fear"* (Luke 21:26, KJV), but he told his disciples not only to look at his wounds but also to touch them. You may see trouble all around you. You may see sickness and problems, but friend, see (with the eyes of your heart) the risen Christ who has the scars to prove who he is!

We don't deny trouble and we affirm the resurrection so our hearts are not overwhelmed by trouble. Don't let your heart be troubled! God is into life! Jesus has risen from the dead. Don't let your heart be troubled by anything! So, what is your problem? What has made your heart skip a beat or two? Jesus has risen from the dead.

Don't just see an empty tomb. See, or understand, that Jesus has risen and touch him with your heart!

MINDS

The mind is a special gift of God. It has the capacity to put knowledge into action. You have been made in the image of God, which is an amazing honor. You can perceive, understand, reason and judge what is true and what is false. Satan likes to place things in your viewer as if they are real and true. A tomb with a torn and broken body was what the disciples imagined with their minds, but earlier Jesus said, *"Destroy this temple, and in three days I will raise it up"* (John 2:19, KJV).

The books of Moses, the prophets and the Psalms all point to Jesus and why he came, so he explained the scriptures to them and their minds were opened. They had an "aha!" moment. Have you ever said something like, "I get it!"? The disciples had that "aha!" moment! They finally understood that Jesus came to defeat death!

Life wins! Death, hell, and the grave were defeated two thousand years ago, so now anyone who commits their lives to Jesus experiences God's gift of eternal life.

Earlier we quoted the apostle Paul from Romans 5:8-9, but let's consider the next verse, *". . .if while when we were enemies we were reconciled to God through the death of His Son, much more, having been reconciled, we shall be saved by His life"* (Romans 5:10, NASB).

Do you remember the newspaper column called "Dear Abby"? One day the column told a story about a young man from a wealthy family who was about to graduate from high school.

It was the custom in that rich neighborhood for the parents to give the graduate a car. "Bill" and his father had spent months looking at cars, and the week before graduation, they found the perfect car. On the eve of his graduation, his father handed him a gift-wrapped Bible. Bill was so angry that he threw the Bible down and stormed out of the house. He and his father never saw each other again. It was the news of his father's death that brought Bill home again. As he sat one night going through his father's possessions that he was to inherit, he come across the Bible his father had given him. He brushed away the dust and opened it to find a cashier's check, dated the day of his graduation—in the exact amount of the car they had chosen together.[10]

Many people have tossed aside the wonderful promise of life because they didn't understand it, or didn't believe that it was possible, but Jesus opens minds to understand what the scriptures say.

---

10 Abigail van Buren, "Modern Parable Teaches Lesson About Gratitude," *Dear Abby* (July 12, 1996), http://www.uexpress.com/dearabby/1996/7/12/modern-parable-teaches-lesson-about-gratitude

The words of Jesus are not only profound—they're personal. They impact every human being.

> *Thus it is written, that the Christ would suffer and rise again from the dead the third day, and that repentance for forgiveness of sins would be proclaimed in His name to all the nations, beginning from Jerusalem.*
> —Luke 24:46-47, NASB

Genesis 3:15, Deuteronomy 18:15, Isaiah 53, and Psalm 16, 22, and 34 are a few instances where Jesus Christ is foretold in the Old Testament, but there are many more. With your mind, see, understand, and grasp that the Son of God, Jesus the Christ, is proclaimed and declared not only in the Old Testament but also throughout the New Testament. It's his story, because God is into life!

- What is the condition of your heart and mind today?
- Is it like the disciples?
- Do you worry about your present and future because of past or present trouble?
- Are you hiding emotionally and intellectually?

Jesus commissioned the disciples to spread the word that judgment and death had been defeated, and that mission has not changed. Now, you and I are entrusted with spreading the good news that Jesus Christ lives and real life is for all of creation to experience because he is risen.

Satan tries to terrorize us with the prospect of death, but God is into life! Look around. Fear of pain and death are Satan's tools to get you and everyone else to doubt the love and power of God, but I proclaim that life is stronger because God is into life. We live in a world of enormous trouble. We don't deny the fact of sin, hate and destruction. We also don't deny that a greater power is at work. *"If the Spirit of Him who raised Jesus from the dead dwells in you, He who raised Christ Jesus from the dead will also give life to your mortal bodies through His Spirit who dwells in you"* (Romans 8:11, NASB).

With this amazing promise made to those who have committed their lives to God—there is no reason to be fearful about the temporary troubles that we face. Remember, Satan and his tactics are not eternal. They have an expiration date. You on the other hand, have eternal life in Jesus when you commit your life to him. So, shake the world with the good news of God's love through the risen Savior. Let your hearts and minds rejoice in life!

chapter six

EIGHT DAYS LATER

But Thomas, one of the twelve, called Didymus, was not with them when Jesus came. So the other disciples were saying to him, "We have seen the Lord!" But he said to them, "Unless I see in His hands the imprint of the nails, and put my finger into the place of the nails, and put my hand into His side, I will not believe."

After eight days His disciples were again inside, and Thomas with them. Jesus came, the doors having been shut, and stood in their midst and said, "Peace be with you." Then He said to Thomas, "Reach here with your finger, and see My hands; and reach here your hand and put it into My side; and do not be unbelieving, but believing." Thomas answered and said to Him, "My Lord and my God!" Jesus said to him, "Because you have seen Me, have you believed? Blessed are they who did not see, and yet believed."

Therefore many other signs Jesus also performed in the presence of the disciples, which are not written in this book; but these have been written so that you may believe that Jesus is the Christ, the Son of God; and that believing you may have life in His name.

After these things Jesus manifested Himself again to the disciples
at the Sea of Tiberias, and He manifested Himself in this way.
—John 20:24-21:1, NASB

When Jesus was betrayed, sadly his disciples didn't support him, but ran and went into hiding. Even at the cross, only one disciple was present. Even after Jesus was resurrected from the dead, we read that the disciples hid for fear of the Jews (John 20:19). They believed Jesus was the Messiah, and Peter even confessed that Jesus was the Son of God (John 6:69), but the testing was furious and they melted under the heat.

Have you ever been tempted and pressured to doubt who Jesus is? You're in good company.

Even those who walked three years with Jesus were shaken by what happened. The significance of Jesus rising from the dead under these conditions cannot be missed.

A grandfather wanted to see how much his four-year-old granddaughter knew about the Resurrection story. He put her on his lap and asked, "Julie, why do we celebrate Easter?" Without hesitating, she said, "Jesus was crucified. After He died, His body was put into a grave. They rolled a big stone in front of the opening. A bunch of soldiers guarded the tomb. On the third day, there was a big earthquake and the stone rolled away." Grandpa was pleased with how much his granddaughter knew about the Resurrection story but then she continued, "When the earthquake happened, the entire town came out by the grave. And if Jesus came out and saw His shadow, they knew there would be six more weeks of winter!" At least she had part of the story right.

The truth is that Jesus is the Risen Savior, the Messiah, and the Son of God. Eight days after the resurrection of Jesus, the disciples met together and a wonderful event happened that reminds us who Jesus is.

JESUS THE RISEN SAVIOR

The apostle Paul wrote that if Jesus did not rise from the dead we are still guilty and condemned (1 Corinthians 15:17). It's easy to distinguish those who believe Jesus rose from the dead from those who don't! Those who do believe have hope! Others don't believe Jesus rose, and they believe this life is all there is! But Jesus said, *"I am the resurrection and the life; he who believes in Me will live even if he dies, and everyone who lives and believes in Me will never die"* (John 11:25-26, NASB).

Live even when you die? What could he have meant by such a statement? Earlier, we learned that life is more than physical. Physical life is not all there is, so even when the body stops, life will continue if belief is placed in the risen Christ.

The problem with Thomas was not doubt but disbelief. Eight days after the resurrection, Thomas met with his friends and he was told the good news that Jesus had defeated death! When Jesus presented himself to the disciples, Jesus had a special message for Thomas: "Do not be doubtful." Jesus also told him that those who believe are happy!

Are you happy today? You believed the testimony of those who were eye witnesses, and because you believe, God has rewarded you with joy! In the twenty-one chapters of the gospel of John, we find the word "believe" ninety-two times. We don't believe in fables and mythical stories, but we do believe the witness of those who saw Jesus physically risen from the dead.

Eight days after the resurrection, Thomas still didn't believe, but after encountering the risen Jesus, he was a changed man! Not only did Thomas make the confession that Jesus is God and Savior, he put action behind his words. Thomas went to India where he told people about the risen Jesus. He eventually gave his life for the gospel.

In his first letter, Peter wrote,

> *Blessed be the God and Father of our Lord Jesus Christ, who according to His great mercy has caused us to be born again to a living hope through the resurrection of Jesus Christ from the dead, to obtain an inheritance which is imperishable and undefiled and will not fade away, reserved in heaven for you, who are protected by the power of God through faith for a salvation ready to be revealed in the last time.*
> —I Peter 1:3-5, NASB

There would be complete despair if Jesus was not raised from the dead. How can we be sure that God has accepted the payment of the blood of Jesus? How do we know beyond a shadow of a doubt that we have been forgiven by God? The Resurrection!

Eight days after the event, Thomas learned to believe that Jesus was risen: Jesus the Messiah. The apostle John wrote that what was written was given so that the reader would believe that Jesus is the Christ (for Jews, the Messiah—John 20:31)

JESUS THE SON OF GOD

People wanted to kill Jesus for saying that he was the Son of God. Best-selling author Tim LaHaye wrote, "Almost everyone who has heard of Jesus has developed an opinion about Him. This is to be expected, for He is not only the most famous person in world history, but also the most controversial."[11] And the famous author, H. G. Wells wrote, "I am an historian, I am not a believer, but I must confess as a historian that this penniless preacher from Nazareth is irrevocably the very center of history. Jesus Christ is easily the most dominant figure in all history."[12] But Jesus, the Son of God? Eight days later, Thomas looked into the eyes of Jesus and said, "My LORD and My God."

"Son" does not always mean that a person was biologically created. There are several ways to be a son. Jeremy Michael Telman is my son by adoption. Ofono Leonard Reck is my son in that he calls me his spiritual father. Leonard is a pastor who planted a church in Uganda, and I have had the joy of mentoring him. Believers are called *sons,* which is a legal term of belonging. There are several ways to be a son. Jesus Christ is uniquely the Son of God not because he was created, but because of his relationship to God the Father. He has always existed. He came to his creation and was born of a virgin

---

11 Tim LaHaye, *Jesus: Who Is He?* (Sisters, Oregon: Multnomah Books, 1996), 59.

12 Pat Williams, *The Paradox of Power: A Transforming View of Leadership,* (Warner Faith Words, 2002).

as was prophesied in Isaiah 7:14. He paid the penalty for the sin of humanity as the perfect sacrifice.

When Thomas said "My LORD and my God," he wasn't talking like people do today when they say "my Lord" or "my God." He wasn't reacting to seeing the wounds on Jesus body. He was believing, which we can tell since his actions thereafter reflected belief. Jesus told him that the person who believes without seeing is happier!

Do you believe that Jesus Christ is the Son of God? He has always been God and one with the Father. He always will be with the Father, but because of his great love for you, he came to bring healing and change your life!

Eight days later, Thomas came to know just who Jesus Christ is! He is the risen Savior who conquered death. He is the Messiah and he is the Son of God who is worthy to be worshipped and served with love and gladness. If Jesus had only come to earth, He would merely have been a visitor. If He had only died, He would merely have been a religious teacher like another Buddha or Mohammed. But He didn't just come to earth, and He didn't just die on a cross. He rose from the dead!

A wonderful hymn, often sung on Easter Sunday, says it best: "He Lives."

Ravi Zacharias wrote, "Sin brings indignity to our essence and pain to our existence. It separates us from God. On the way to the cross 2,000 years ago, Jesus took the ultimate indignity and the ultimate pain to bring us the dignity of a relationship with God and the healing of our souls."[13]

When Jesus said, "God so loved the world," he proved it by rising from the dead. Even though it has been stated previously, let me once again ask, have you ever said you were sorry to someone and they didn't accept your apology, as if it made no difference? When Jesus was crucified and raised, God received us as if we had never sinned. Those who will commit their very lives to God in faith will receive the greatest gift of all: eternal life found in the very presence of the creator.

Eight days later Thomas came to know just who Jesus is! He's the risen Savior who conquered death! He is the Messiah and he is the Son of God who is worthy to be worshipped and served with love and gladness!

---

13 Ravi Zacharias, posted on Facebook on April 10, 2014.

chapter seven

MORE ON HIS MIND

Before the Passover celebration, Jesus knew that his hour had come to leave this world and return to his Father. He had loved his disciples during his ministry on earth, and now he loved them to the very end. It was time for supper, and the devil had already prompted Judas, son of Simon Iscariot, to betray Jesus. Jesus knew that the Father had given him authority over everything and that he had come from God and would return to God. So he got up from the table, took off his robe, wrapped a towel around his waist, and poured water into a basin. Then he began to wash the disciples' feet, drying them with the towel he had around him.
—John 13:1-5, NLT

Israel was to remind itself of God's deliverance from the hundreds of years of bondage that they had been under in Egypt by observing the Passover. The command of God for the Jews to celebrate Passover is found in Deuteronomy 16:12 and Exodus 12:14. We read that before the Feast of Passover, Jesus and his disciples met. They met to eat, but Jesus had more on his mind.

In the above passage, we learn three things about Jesus Christ.

JESUS KNOWS

Before this moment, Jesus knew that the time for him to give his life for a sinful humanity had not come. In fact, there were several times that his enemies wanted to kill him but could not because Jesus had more to do (John 7:30). John 8:6 (NASB) records that the scribes and Pharisees tested Jesus, *"so that they might have grounds for accusing Him."* They were trying to catch him, but until this moment they were not able to condemn him to death, even though they were thinking it. But now Jesus said, *"The hour has come for the Son of Man to be glorified"* (John 12:23, NASB).

It's obvious that it was not honorable to be crucified. It was a criminal's death. Jesus Christ, who is 100% God and 100% man, knew that excruciating pain was about to happen.

He said, *"Now judgement is upon this world; now the ruler of this world will be cast out. And I, if I am lifted up from the earth, will draw all men to Myself"* (John 12:31-32, NASB). The verb used for "lifted up" (the ancient Greek word *hypsothenai*) has a deliberate double meaning. It means both a literal elevation (as in being raised up on a cross) and exaltation (being raised in honor).

Here, Jesus isn't talking about us "lifting him up" through worship. He was "lifted up" on the cross, and we proclaim that fact to the world. We lift Jesus up by witnessing, presenting and preaching Christ (I Corinthians 1:23). To the people of that day, they knew that "being lifted up" meant crucifixion.

Earlier, Jesus plainly told his disciples, *"Behold, we are going up to Jerusalem; and the Son of Man will be delivered to the chief priests and scribes, and they will condemn Him to death, and will hand Him over to the Gentiles*

[Romans] to mock and scourge and crucify Him, and on the third day He will be raised up" (Matthew 20:18-19, NASB).

Jesus knew what was going to happen. He not only knew about what was ahead for him, he knew what was going to happen to his disciples. Jesus told them, *"All of you will desert me. For the Scriptures say, 'God will strike the Shepherd, and the sheep will be scattered'"* (Mark 4:27, NLT, quoting Zechariah 13:7). Not only did Jesus know what was about to happen to himself and to his disciples, he also knew about you and me. He knew that we would sin and would turn away from his love.

The Psalmist said, *"Your faithfulness extends to every generation, as enduring as the earth you created"* (Psalm 119:90, NLT).

The beauty of God's knowledge is expressed in a song that was popular many years ago: "When He was on the Cross." It seems like a cute statement, but the truth is that he knew you and he knew me. His knowledge of us all can only be attributed to the fact that he is the very creator.

Jesus knew who you would be before you were born; he also knew that you would choose to turn away from him, and yet he loved you.

JESUS LOVES

The love that Jesus Christ had for his disciples was *agape*. That is 100% giving of self.

It's the kind of love that is unconditional, self-sacrificing, active, volitional, and thoughtful. Matthew gives more details about the last supper. Jesus said that one of the disciples would betray him and they all asked, *"Am I the one, Lord?"* (Matthew 26:22, NLT). Jesus' answer shows how much he loved. He said, *"He who dipped his hand with Me in the bowl is the one who will betray Me"* (Matthew 26:23, NASB).

When Jesus said this, he was not pointing out one specific disciple, because they all dipped bread with him. Instead, Jesus was identifying the betrayer as a friend, someone who ate at the same table with Him, someone who he loved.

Jesus showed love for Judas, even knowing his treachery. That's the love of God. Even though he knew that we would turn our backs on him in sin, he loved us. Romans 5:8 (NASB) says, *"God demonstrates His own love toward us, in that while we were yet sinners, Christ died for us."* And further, *"God showed how much he loved us by sending his one and only Son into the world so that we might have eternal life through him. This is real love—not that we loved God, but that he loved us and sent his Son as a sacrifice to take away our sins"* (I John 4:9-10, NASB).

Judas chose to turn away from the love of God but Jesus loved him, just as he loves all who have ever lived. Still, we can resist his wonderful love by excluding him from our lives or by minimizing his greatness. The love of Jesus is *agape*. He gave everything so that you and I might have life (*zoe*) and that more abundantly forever. His love is an amazing servant love.

JESUS SERVES

Notice what Jesus did after eating with his disciples: he served them by washing their feet.

Washing the feet of a guest was the job of a servant, but Jesus performed this task, seeing that it had not been done by anyone.

Imagine—Jesus knew what was about to happen, but he had time to serve his disciples.

I want you to know that God is not too busy to care for you. The humility of Jesus Christ is breathtaking! He told the disciples, *". . . whoever wishes to be first among you shall be slave of all. For even the Son of Man did not come to be served, but to serve, and to give His life a ransom for many"* (Mark 10:44-45, NASB).

He also said that *"I gave you an example that you also should do as I did to you"* (John 13:15, NASB), but they did not fully grasp the significance of what he did when he stooped down and served them. Foot-washing is a dramatic allegory of the sin-cleansing death of Christ. Its spiritual meaning: Jesus, the divine Lord, made himself nothing—he became a human being, he took our sin upon himself in his death, and by that death he washes away our sin. But like Peter, our human pride does not want to permit this. Some may think that they can be cleansed of sin by other means, but Jesus says to all: Unless I wash away your sin, you have no part with me. Jesus realized that the disciples did not understand the spiritual significance of what he had just done. (John 13:7, 12).

The disciples would understand only later, after his death and resurrection. If this incident was just about foot-washing and humble service it would have been understandable there and then; it would not have needed the clarifying events of Christ's death and resurrection. This also reminds us that service alone is not what will cleanse the guilt of sin. It is sad, but some serve others thinking that their good works will be enough. Jesus made it clear that he served by giving himself up for each and every one. The deep spiritual meaning of the foot washing—the forgiveness of sin—is what Jesus is commanding us to copy, to imitate. Not that we can cleanse the sin of another, but if Jesus, the Holy One of God, against whom we have offended utterly, has forgiven us, then we can also forgive.

Jesus had more on his mind when he went for supper that night. Jesus knows, loves and serves, but the message that we celebrate and tell others is that Jesus Christ rose from the dead and lives today. If you tell people about the risen Christ, they may not believe you. They may even think you are crazy. Well, you are in good company.

In the book of Acts, we read that many scoffed when Paul told the Greeks in Athens that Jesus rose from the dead (Acts 17:32). The good news is that there will be some who believe quickly, and others will want to hear more. We don't preach church or rules but a risen savior. As we celebrate what Jesus did, we must keep in mind that Jesus Christ is not dead. The tombs of Mohammed and Buddha contain their ashes, but the tomb Jesus' body was laid in is empty. Jesus had you and the rest of humanity on his mind. He knew, he loved and he served. He was crucified and he rose, and that is what we celebrate today.

chapter eight

DESTRUCTION AND RESURRECTION

The Passover of the Jews was near, and Jesus went up to Jerusalem. And He found in the temple those who were selling oxen and sheep and doves, and the money changers seated at their tables. And He made a scourge of cords, and drove them all out of the temple, with the sheep and the oxen; and He poured out the coins of the money changers and overturned their tables; and to those who were selling the doves He said, "Take these things away; stop making My Father's house a place of business." His disciples remembered that it was written, "Zeal for Your house will consume me." The Jews then said to Him, "What sign do You show us as your authority for doing these things?" Jesus answered them, "Destroy this temple, and in three days I will raise it up." The Jews then said, "It took forty-six years to build this temple, and will You raise it up in three days?" But He was speaking of the temple of His body. So when He was raised from the dead, His disciples remembered that He said this; and they believed the Scripture and the word which Jesus had spoken. Now when He was in Jerusalem at the Passover, during the feast, many believed in His name, observing His signs which He was doing.

—John 2:13-23, NASB

The scene: people are coming and going into the temple in Jerusalem, while Jesus is driving out merchants who were making a big buck, but had no interest in people meeting with God. So, the Jews questioned him and asked, "What sign do You show us as your authority for doing these things?" In other words, they were saying, "Who gave you the right to do this?" They were certainly not ready to hear the Lord's reply, for He said, "Destroy this temple, and in three days I will raise it up." It is interesting that Jesus gave a response that reflected the fact that the many of the Jew would hate Him and seek His life.

The Temple in Jesus' day was referred to as the "Second Temple." Solomon's Temple was destroyed by the Babylonians in 586 B.C. Seventy years later a new Temple was built in Jerusalem. Jesus was saying that they would most certainly see a sign. The sign he would give them that would authenticate who he was would be his resurrection from the dead. It wouldn't be turning water into wine or healing the blind or feeding five thousand or calming the storm or walking on the water, but it would be the very last sign: his resurrection. Jesus made it clear that though some would destroy his body, he would raise himself up. The Jews didn't get it; in fact, at his trial, they said, *"This man stated, 'I am able to destroy the temple of God and to rebuild it in three days'"* (Matthew 26:61, NASB).

The resurrection of Jesus Christ shows us that he does have authority, that he is the life and that he is the speaker of truth.

THE AUTHORITY

The resurrection happened! As was stated earlier, there are many documented instances where someone was brought back to life after dying, but Jesus Christ is the one who conquered death. Lazarus was resurrected, but then he died again. However, Jesus raised himself and lives even today! His authority over death comes from the fact that he has all power and nothing can possibly oppose him and win. The sign that he gave was his greatest and his last sign, proving his authority to cleanse the temple.

Jesus entered the temple at another time not to cleanse it but to teach. In Matthew 21:23 we read that Jesus was again questioned about his authority. This time he challenged the thinking of the chief priests and the elders. Since they would not be honest, he told them that he would not reveal by what authority he did things. On another occasion, Jesus was teaching and people *"were astonished at his doctrine: for he taught them as one that had authority"* (Mark 1:22, KJV).

Jesus Christ is the authority—not Oprah, not commercials, not friends, and that is why the wise will know what he says and will be obedient to it. Jesus said,

> *I tell you the truth, those who listen to my message and believe in God who sent me have eternal life. They will never be condemned for their sins, but they have already passed from death into life.*
>
> *And I assure you that the time is coming, indeed it's here now, when the dead will hear my voice—the voice of the Son of God. And those who listen will live. The Father has life in himself, and he has*

*granted that same life-giving power to his Son. And he has given him
authority to judge everyone because he is the Son of Man.*

—John 5:24-27, NLT

Jesus also has the authority to forgive sins. Man's deepest need
is not for fairness, but for forgiveness. Forgiveness is the power to
liberate from past sin and restore to an individual a sense of self-
worth. Forgiveness is the power to deal with justifiable guilt, not
by ignoring it, but by eliminating it. Forgiveness is a cool drink of
water to a dry and parched tongue. It is the medicine which heals
us at the deepest level of our being. We all need forgiveness. Jesus
verified his authority to forgive when he gave his life up as a sacrifice.
He didn't just say "I forgive you," his actions proved that he forgave.

Jesus Christ is the final authority on all things. We can either
go to him and live, or we can rebel and do our own thing, but the
result will be disastrous because he is the life.

THE LIFE

Earlier, we mentioned one Greek word for life that is found in the
New Testament. The Greek words *bios*, *psyche* and *zoe* are translated
"life" in the New Testament. Did you know there is more to life
than what you see?

- *Bios* is the root of the word "biology" that we use to
  describe physical life.
- *Psyche* describes the life of the mind, thought and per-
  sonality.

- *Zoe* is the most common word for life in the New Testament. It is the spiritual life that one has because of being in relationship with the creator.

Watch how life is described in terms of relationship to God.

- "In Him was life (*zoe*), and the life (*zoe*) was the light of men." (John 1:4, NASB)
- "I am the way, and the truth, and the life (*zoe*)." (John 14:6, NASB)
- "I came that they might have life (*zoe*), and have it abundantly." (John 10:10, NLT)
- "...these [things] have been written that you might believe that Jesus is the Christ, the Son of God; and that believing you may have life (*zoe*) in His name." (John 20:31, NASB)
- "He who has the Son has the life (*zoe*); he who does not have the Son of God does not have the life (*zoe*)." (1 John 5:12, NASB)

The author of the *Chronicles of Narnia*, C.S. Lewis, wrote, "the biological sort of life which comes to us through Nature, and which (like everything else in Nature) is always tending to run down and decay so that it can only be kept up air, water, food, etc., is *Bios*."[14]

---

14 C.S. Lewis, *The Joyful Christian* (Touchstone, 1996), 41.

The spiritual life which is in God from all eternity, and which made the whole natural universe, is *zoe*.

Bios has, to be sure, a certain shadowy or symbolic resemblance to *zoe*, but only the sort of resemblance there is between a photo and a place, or a statue and a man. A man who changed from having *bios* to having *zoe* would have gone through as big a change as a statue which changed from being a carved stone to being a real man.

We are not begotten by God, we are only made by Him; in our natural state, we are not sons of God, only (so to speak) statues. We do not have *zoe* or spiritual life: only *bios* or biological life which is presently going to run down and die. The whole offer which Christianity makes is this: that we can, if we let God have His way, come to share in the life of Christ. If we do, we shall then be sharing a life which was begotten, not made, which always has existed and always will exist. Christ is the Son of God. If we share in this kind of life we also shall be sons of God. Jesus said, *"I am the resurrection and the life; he who believes in Me will live even if he dies, and everyone who lives and believes in Me will never die"* (John 11:25-26, NASB).

God made you a living soul. There is much more to you than just the *bios*. Paul the apostle wrote the Ephesian church and said,

> . . .*you were dead in your trespasses and sins, in which you formerly walked according to the course of this world, according to the prince of the power of the air, of the spirit that is now working in the sons of disobedience. Among them we too all formerly lived in the lusts of our flesh, indulging the desires of the flesh and of the mind, and were by nature children of wrath, even as the rest. But God, being rich in mercy, because of His great love with which He loved us, even when*

Destruction and Resurrection

*we were dead in our transgressions, made us alive together with Christ
... and raised us up with Him...*

—Ephesians 2:1-6, NASB

Some may have *bios* but actually be dead. Jesus Christ rose and gives *zoe* to those who commit their lives to him. The body is temporary, but the real "you" is created to live on past the grave. Either it will be with the creator God or in judgement. That's why we live for God and not for the flesh. *"...God so loved the world, that He gave His only begotten Son, that whoever believes in Him shall not perish, but have eternal life"* (John 3:16, NASB). Jesus is the resurrection and the life!

THE SPEAKER OF TRUTH

Some have boldly proclaimed, "Jesus said it, I believe it and that settles it!" To a culture that celebrates the idea of not knowing what truth is, the Psalmist said, *"Lead me in thy truth, and teach me: for thou art the God of my salvation; on thee do I wait all the day"* (Psalm 25:5, KJV). In reality, truth is desired and so we daily pursue it. Without it, everything falls apart. The disciples understood this lesson: *"...when He was raised from the dead, His disciples remembered that He said this; and they believed the Scripture and the word which Jesus had spoken"* (John 2:22, NASB).

Postmodernist philosophers claim that truth is relative. They often say, "That may be true for you" or "We shouldn't judge." Such an attitude applied to medicine or science would be ridiculous. Satan started the ball rolling in the Garden of Eden when he questioned the truthfulness of God, but what God says is truth.

The first prophecy given was from God. He said to Satan, *"...I will cause hostility between you and the woman, and between your offspring and her offspring. He will strike your head, and you will strike his heel"* (Genesis 3:15, NLT). Through Jesus Christ, Satan was given a fatal blow. He thought he had won with the death of the Son of God, but on that morning, Satan, death and the grave were defeated!

God does not lie! You may not see it now. It may be down the road, but what God says will happen! After the resurrection, the disciples remembered what Jesus said and then they believed.

When Jesus said, "Destroy this temple," most likely pointing to his own body, and "In three days, I will raise it up," he was telling the truth. It happened!

So, if he says that he loves you, does he love you? If he says that he will provide for you, will he provide? If he says that he will make a way, will he make a way? Jesus is the speaker of truth. *"He himself bore our sins in His body on the cross, so that we might die to sin and live to righteousness..."* (I Peter 2:24, NASB). Jesus Christ is the living Son of God who is the authority and speaks the truth. Let's worship him!

chapter nine

AN AMAZING ROAD TRIP

That same day two of Jesus' followers were walking to the village of Emmaus, seven miles from Jerusalem. As they walked along they were talking about everything that had happened. As they talked and discussed these things, Jesus himself suddenly came and began walking with them. But God kept them from recognizing him.

He asked them, "What are you discussing so intently as you walk along?"

They stopped short, sadness written across their faces. Then one of them, Cleopas, replied, "You must be the only person in Jerusalem who hasn't heard about all the things that have happened there the last few days."

"What things?" Jesus asked.

"The things that happened to Jesus, the man from Nazareth," they said. "He was a prophet who did powerful miracles, and he was a mighty teacher in the eyes of God and all the people. But our leading priests and other religious leaders handed him over to be condemned to death, and they crucified him. We had hoped he was the Messiah who had come to rescue Israel. This all happened three days ago.

"Then some women from our group of his followers were at his tomb early this morning, and they came back with an amazing report. They said his body was missing, and they had seen angels who told them Jesus is alive! Some of our men ran out to see, and sure enough, his body was gone, just as the women had said."

Then Jesus said to them, "You foolish people! You find it so hard to believe all that the prophets wrote in the Scriptures. Wasn't it clearly predicted that the Messiah would have to suffer all these things before entering his glory?" Then Jesus took them through the writings of Moses and all the prophets, explaining from all the Scriptures the things concerning himself.

By this time they were nearing Emmaus and the end of their journey. Jesus acted as if he were going on, but they begged him, "Stay the night with us, since it is getting late." So he went home with them. As they sat down to eat, he took the bread and blessed it. Then he broke it and gave it to them. Suddenly, their eyes were opened, and they recognized him. And at that moment he disappeared!

They said to each other, "Didn't our hearts burn within us as he talked with us on the road and explained the Scriptures to us?"

—Luke 24:13-32, NLT

Carole and I have driven the length and breadth of North America, but there was an amazing road trip that took place in the first century. The crucifixion happened and Sunday came! Jesus rose from the dead and he presented himself to his people, but two hadn't seen Jesus yet. Cleopas and an unnamed friend were on a road trip to Emmaus, which was 11 km northwest of Jerusalem.

They were going on with life. The life of Jesus and the hope of change had been great but, oh well, change didn't happen. Roman was still ruthlessly persecuting Israel. Isn't that a little like our lives? Jesus came, he gave himself for our sins. It's a great story, but life goes on, right?

The truth is that life is hard. Even though Jesus died for our sins and he rose from the dead, we still have trouble to deal with. We still get colds. We still have disappointments. We still battle fear, worry and temptation. But there are two important truths that scripture shows us in Luke 24.

First: Life is not the same since Jesus rose from the dead.

Second: He wants us to see with our eyes, hearts and minds.

JESUS BRINGS CHANGE

When Jesus died on the cross, some were tempted to think that life was going to remain the same, but the truth was that everything had changed. The worst possible response to the fact of the resurrection is to live like it never happened. Jesus called the two foolish and slow of heart to believe.

They shouldn't have actually needed Jesus to show himself to them for them to have believed. God had told mankind what was going to happen through the prophets.

The sad fact is that these two were followers of Jesus. They were saved but lived like the resurrection didn't happen. Jesus told them, it was necessary for the Christ to suffer and then to enter into glory. The enormity of our sin made it necessary for Jesus to suffer.

We can never minimize how awful our sin is, but Jesus changes life and we live our lives in the fact of the resurrection!

Things are different now because of the resurrection. We don't walk through life on our own with an "oh well" kind of attitude. We live with the assurance of eternal life because God has said so.

When Jesus was walking with the two men on the road to Emmaus, they said to him, *"...we were hoping that it was He who was going to redeem Israel"* (Luke 24:21, NASB). They were only looking for freedom from the Romans, but Jesus came to do more than to free us from our physical troubles. He came to free us from death that resulted from sin. Jesus changes life!

A man named JD tells the wonderful story of how Jesus changes lives.

> I had been addicted to drugs for many years and had completely given up hope of ever being free. While in a hotel room paid for by a local charity I laid down on the bed next to my six-week-old baby. He looked like an angel sleeping there next to me. I smiled, briefly imagining the happy life he would have without me. I knew that someone would be there soon to clean the room, and he would be safe. That's when I decided to take my own life. Someone started yelling at me. "Hey, you, you heroin addict lying there in that hotel room, don't you know that God loves you, don't you know that Jesus wants to change your life?" I hadn't noticed that the TV was on but when I turned to look at it there was a man on the screen yelling and pointing his finger at me. I had no idea

what he meant but somewhere deep in my soul the will
to live was stirred by that message. Five months later,
by divine appointment in a pastor's office, I understood.
The pastor told me about Jesus. He told me that God
loved me and had a plan for my life. He explained how I
could have a relationship with God, about how Jesus had
paid the debt I owed God for my sins by dying on a cross
in my place. In my mind's eye, I could see a cross on a
hill. In front of the cross there were many roads winding
in every direction. I knew they were the paths and roads
I had been on throughout my life. All the roads ended
at the same place, and that was at the foot of the cross.
I could see that in the distance, on the other side of the
cross, there were only two roads, two choices. I asked
God to forgive my sins, and surrendered my life to Jesus.
That was 19 years ago. Jesus truly changed my life, He
gave me a life worth living.[15]

We don't walk through life as if the resurrection didn't happen! We live in faith and belief in him who was promised! Like the
two on the road, Thomas hadn't seen Jesus yet, so he said he would
not believe the resurrection unless he could touch the wounds in
Jesus' hands and side. So, when Jesus presented himself to Thomas
he said, *"You believe because you have seen me. Blessed* [makarios—*happy or*

---

15 From the defunct website "Jesus Changed My Life."

favored] are those who believe without seeing me" (John 20:29, NLT). We believe and are happy though we have not seen him in the flesh yet.

The parents of Braun were agnostics, but they felt that at least once in his life, he ought to go to church. So, they took him. That Sunday, the pastor preached about the crucifixion of a man. He described the nails driven through the man's hands, the crown of thorns jammed upon his head, the blood that ran down his face, and the spear that ripped into his side. He described the agony in his eyes and the sorrow in his voice when he prayed, "Father, forgive them, for they do not know what they are doing." Halfway through the sermon, little Braun was crying. Wouldn't somebody do something? Wouldn't the congregation rise up together and take the man down from the cross? But as he looked around in astonished surprise, he saw that the people were complacent. "What's the matter with these people, Mom?" he asked. "Why doesn't somebody do something about that man on the cross?" Patting Braun on the shoulder, his mother nervously whispered in reply, "Braun, Braun, be quiet. It's just a story. Don't let it trouble you. Just listen quietly. You'll soon forget about this old story when we go home."

Is the crucifixion simply a story? What about the resurrection? Is it only a story to be forgotten as we walk through life, or are lives changed as the believer walks with Jesus? The Psalmist David wrote, *"The Lord is my shepherd; I have all that I need. He lets me rest in green meadows; he leads me beside peaceful streams. He renews my strength. He guides me along right paths, bringing honor to his name. Even when I walk through the darkest valley, I will not be afraid, for you are close beside me"* (Psalm 23:1-4, NLT).

Though we don't see him, we believe that Jesus Christ is with us no matter where we walk in this life. This changes how we choose to live. And the faith that we place in him releases his touch upon our lives. Remember, the worst possible response to the fact of the resurrection is to live like it never happened. When we believe in the resurrected Christ, change happens. We possess joy, peace and the assurance of a glorious future. Jesus changes lives from despair and fear.

JESUS OPENS OUR EYES

Jesus walked with two apostles who did not have eyes to see that the living Christ was walking with them. It's sad and amazing that they could not recognize Jesus. Jesus was someone they knew, but doubt clouded their eyes. Sometimes perceptions can be incorrect. Assumptions are often misleading, if not downright wrong. We tend to judge ourselves by our intent, but we judge others by their behavior.

Since we don't know others' intent, we should always assume the best. One mistake that most people commonly make is that they assume things before they know what is true.

Even though there were many prophecies of the resurrection and the apostles had found no body, the men on the road said to Jesus, *"Some women from our group of his followers were at his tomb early this morning, and they came back with an amazing report. They said his body was missing, and they had seen angels who told them Jesus is alive! Some of our men ran out to see, and sure enough, his body was gone, just as the women had said"* (Luke 24:22-24, NLT). They saw but they didn't see. God wants us to see with our eyes, hearts and minds. God's incomparably great power is available for those who believe.

Paul wrote, *"I pray that the eyes of your heart may be enlightened, so that you will know what is the hope of His calling, what are the riches of the glory of*

His inheritance in the saints and what is the surpassing greatness of His power toward us who believe" (Ephesians 1:18-19, NASB). If you don't want to see the truth, you will not accept the resurrection, but God will continue to affect your life with who he is.

Philip Yancey tells the story of George Buttrick, former chaplain at Harvard. Buttrick recalled that students would come into his office, plop down on a chair and declare, "I don't believe in God." He responded by saying "tell me what kind of God you don't believe in. I probably don't believe in that God either."[16] And then he would talk about Jesus Christ, the risen Son of God. You see, Jesus corrects our assumptions about God.

> *For it was the Father's good pleasure for all the fullness to dwell in Him, and through Him to reconcile all things to Himself, having made peace through the blood of His cross; through Him, I say, whether things on earth or things in heaven.*
>
> —Colossians 1:19-20, NASB

As Jesus continued to explain what the prophets had said what would happen, these two felt something in their hearts. They gave into the fire of the truth and they suddenly saw that this one on the road trip with them was none other than Jesus Christ himself. Their eyes were opened! They believed what Jesus said and they saw that it was him! Jesus opens the eyes of the spiritually blind as we place our faith in him!

---

16 Philip Yancey, *The Jesus I Never Knew* (Grand Rapids, MI: Zondervan, 2008).

Right now, where you are, say it out loud: *"I lift my eyes to you, O God, enthroned in heaven. We keep looking to the Lord our God for his mercy"* (Psalm 123:1-2, NLT). On your road trip through life, remember that Jesus Christ is risen and by his spirit he walks alongside you. Through sickness, loss, pain, challenges, and fears, through storms and attacks of the enemy, you are not alone! He is risen!

With Paul, again, *"I pray that the eyes of your heart may be enlightened, so that you will know what is the hope of His calling, what are the riches of the glory of His inheritance in the saints, and what is the surpassing greatness of His power toward us who believe"* (Ephesians 1:18-19, NASB).

He was crucified and he rose. He ascended to the Father and will physically return to receive those who are eagerly awaiting him.

chapter ten

DEBT-FREE

When the fulness of the time was come, God sent forth his Son, made of a woman, made under the law, to redeem them that were under the law, that we might receive the adoption of sons. And because ye are sons, God hath sent forth the Spirit of his Son into your hearts, crying, Abba, Father. Wherefore thou art no more a servant, but a son; and if a son, then an heir of God through Christ.

—Galatians 4:4-7, KJV

Debt is a real issue. It's when you owe. Owing is commonly thought of in dollars and cents, but it's much more than money. The Bible says that debt is a source of pain. It's a pain for me. It's a pain for you. Fortunately, the Bible has a lot to say about how we can deal with this kind of pain. Next to love, debt is the most common topic in the Bible. Debt will eventually result in death, but Jesus conquered death when he rose from the grave. The result is that anyone can be debt-free.

When Jesus began his ministry, he said that his ministry was good news for the poor. He "proclaimed release to the captives," implying that people would be freed from various sorts of bondage, whether economic, physical, emotional or demonic. He lets "the oppressed go free" (Luke 4:18-19).

The elite have always used debt to press their advantages and to imperil the lives of others. Jesus saw debt differently. Jesus viewed debt as an opportunity for forgiveness. God does not demand repayment for every last penny of indebtedness; instead, God offers abundant mercy. Debts would be forgiven without any kind of payment. God is not a God who maintained debt records for foreclosing on the poor. He's a God who canceled debt and restored real life (*zoe*). God has paid the expense of our sinfulness and has offered a debt-free life. Our response, then, is to live a debt-free life—owing nothing but love.

GOD THE FATHER SENT THE SON

Since we all sold ourselves to sin and destruction, God, in his love and mercy, sent the son, because he forgives debt. Paul had to explain to the Galatian Christians what the purpose of the law was, because some of them were being told that if they wanted to go to heaven they had to keep rules.

Have you heard, or perhaps even believed, the same thing? "If I'm good and don't break the law (too much) I will go to heaven."

Paul explained to them when and why God gave them the law. The law was introduced after God had given the promise of the Savior, as a *paidagogos*. A *paidagogos* was the slave who was sent to be with a schoolboy to make sure that he didn't get into trouble on the way to school and got there safely.

As the Israelites lived, they began straying further and further away from God, so God sent the law through Moses, as a sort of "big brother" to look over the Israelites—to keep them in line. The law kept on condemning Israel, so they looked forward to a Savior. The law kept Israel separate, so they could have the Savior through their race. The law kept the Israel from going too far astray from God. God ultimately wanted Israelite believers to be living in Israel so the Savior could be born through them. The history of the Israelites shows that they went through a lot. The law did its job. When Israel broke the law, they went into captivity. They were punished. But finally, after two different captivities under the Assyrians and the Babylonians, a remnant was left surviving under foreign rule in the land of Israel. It wasn't exactly the way it should or could have been from a physical standpoint. But in God's eyes, the time was right. It was time to send his Son. The law did its job and showed that sin throws us into debt, but God sent the Son to free mankind.

GOD PAID THE DEBT WE OWED (VERSE 5)

Redeeming something, especially something that someone else sold to a pawn shop, is a merciful act. In the Bible, sometimes people would get into such great debt that they would become servants. In other words, they made an agreement to work a certain number of years to pay off a debt.

Sometimes their debt would be so great that they would end up working for someone for their entire lives, never to truly be free again. Jesus came to "redeem those under law" by being born "under the law." The law had many demands.

79

- Don't lie.
- Don't covet your neighbor's house, even if it's better than yours.
- Don't hate.
- Don't lust.

And many more! And if you broke just one law, you deserved hell. *"The wages of sin is death, but the free gift of God is eternal life in Christ Jesus our LORD"* (Romans 6:23, NASB).

God paid what we owed with something very precious and worth more than anything in this world.

> *If you address as Father the One who impartially judges according to each one's work, conduct yourselves in fear during the time of your stay on earth; knowing that you were not redeemed with perishable things like silver or gold from your futile way of life inherited from your forefathers, but with precious blood, as of a lamb unblemished and spotless, the blood of Christ.*
>
> —I Peter 1:17-19, NASB

In 1994, Carole I and bought a house in Kansas City. Every two weeks we made a payment, but we were still in debt. Imagine if some wealthy person had paid the debt off for us but we continued to pay the bank. The bank would gladly continue to take the payment, but if we knew the debt was already paid that would be foolish, wouldn't it?

The apostle Paul is saying the same thing in Galatians 4. In fact, in chapter 3, he calls the Galatians foolish for believing that they needed to earn their way to heaven. Your good works are woefully insufficient to pay your debt. There is only one payment that is precious enough to pay what you owe, and that is the precious blood of the sinless Son of God.

God has paid off your debt and you are debt-free because of his love for you, expressed in the gift of Jesus sacrificed on the cross. What you and I must do is repent and accept this gift; otherwise we will be foolish, still paying off a debt that has already been paid.

GOD MADE US SONS (VERSE 7)

No longer are we called and treated like slaves because of the resurrection of Jesus. We are legal heirs because of faith in this God of love. The apostle Paul uses the same word here for God as he does in Romans 8:14-17. Paul calls "Daddy." He's more than "Father." There is an intimacy that we have with the creator because of adoption. Adoption means that you are legally a child of God. Welcome to God's family!

At the time of this letter to the Galatian church, the word adoption was used differently than we use it today. When we speak about adoption today, we are talking about taking a child that is not our own flesh and blood, and legally making them our own. That's what Carole and I did in 1988 when we became Jeremy's parents. However, that is not the Biblical meaning of adoption.

Understand that the Romans and the Greeks had a ceremony they went through with their own flesh-and-blood children. That ceremony was called adoption, which literally means "the placing of a son." If a child was under the legal age of inheritance, they were not really considered to be a full-fledged member of the family. They did not enjoy all the rights and privileges of family membership.

When they became an adult, that is, reached the legal age of inheritance, they went through a ceremony called the *toga virilis.* They would take the toga off the back of the adult, place it on the back of the child, and then pronounce them to be a full-fledged member of the family, with all the according rights and privileges. Welcome to the family!

As an heir to the creator and sustainer of life, you are debt-free because of who God is! He sent the Son, paid your debt and has made you a legal heir to his riches. Remember, debt and riches, like life, are much more than simply physical because you are more than a body.

Jesus presents repentance in the context not of fear but of joy. Some may teach that we should turn to God because he's angry and will destroy us otherwise, but Jesus taught us to turn because God is love. Salvation is the dynamic of mercy, of love without limit, of welcome and generosity.

> *Oh give thanks to the Lord, for He is good, For His lovingkindness is everlasting. Let the redeemed of the Lord say so, Whom He has redeemed from the hand of the adversary.*
>
> —Psalm 107:1-3, NASB

Now that you are debt-free, live that way! The resurrection of Jesus proves that you're debt-free. Later today, read Galatians chapter 5. Paul issues a warning: *"You were called to freedom, brethren; only do not turn your freedom into an opportunity for the flesh, but through love serve one another"* (Galatians 5:13, NASB). How foolish it would be to become a slave to creditors after being set free! Paul reminds us to prove we are free by loving others. If you are debt-free, owe nothing but love; Jesus not only died, he rose.

chapter eleven

A CONTRASTING PICTURE OF JESUS

...I saw heaven opened, and behold, a white horse, and He who sat on it is called Faithful and True, and in righteousness He judges and wages war. His eyes are a flame of fire, and on His head are many diadems; and He has a name written on Him which no one knows except Himself. He is clothed with a robe dipped in blood, and His name is called The Word of God. And the armies which are in heaven, clothed in fine linen, white and clean, were following Him on white horses. From His mouth comes a sharp sword, so that with it He may strike down the nations, and He will rule them with a rod of iron; and He treads the wine press of the fierce wrath of God, the Almighty. And on His robe and on His thigh He has a name written, "King of Kings, and Lord of Lords."

—Revelation 19:11-16, NASB

Crucifixion is the most brutal torture that man has ever carried out. Jesus entered Jerusalem to the celebration of crowds. They saw him heal blind eyes, cleanse lepers, raise the dead and miraculously provide food for thousands, but on a horrible date in mankind's history, Jesus was forsaken, beaten and crucified. We have documented and detailed accounts about this tragic event. We also have the empty tomb, and the witness of many that Jesus rose from the dead as had been prophesied.

Contrasting the picture of Jesus beaten, bloody, wearing a crown of thorns and being mocked is what we read in Revelation 19:11-16. When Jesus was crucified, the average person would have seen defeat, but he came to save the world from judgment. Jesus said, *"God did not send the Son into the world to judge the world, but that the world might be saved through Him"* (John 3:17, NASB). Jesus Christ is the prince of peace. He resisted the idea that the Messiah would be a military ruler that would crush the evil Romans, but his disciples tried to correct him when he told them that he came to die (Mark 8:31-32). Imagine correcting Jesus Christ! He came to bring peace to a sin-sick world, but when we read Revelation 19, we see Jesus on a white horse, wearing a kingly crown, wearing a robe (not stripped), with a sharp sword coming from his mouth and with his name written on his thigh.

When we want to try to convey some abstract thought, we often put it in symbolic form. The New Testament was originally written in Greek. Greek thought is abstract, with concepts that are represented by words such as "grace" and "salvation," but Hebrew thought is concrete, assisting the reader's understanding through symbolism. You'll find passages where God is described as having feathers (Psalm 91:4). The word angry is an abstract word that needs explanation, but in Hebrew, it literally means "nose." When angry the nose flares so representing anger as an actual physical sign is a concrete physical way to understand. Even though the New

Testament is abstract, many of the writers, including Matthew, Peter, Paul and John, were Jews who conveyed messages in concrete terms in addition to the abstract. Revelation is a picture book to help us understand future events. It was written in a way that many generations could understand. You might ask, "Is Revelation literal or figurative, then?" The answer is both. As we study it, we will see why John saw things the way he did.

JESUS ON A WHITE HORSE

When Jesus triumphantly entered Jerusalem, he was riding a colt, but in Revelation 19 he is on a white horse. A horse was used for war and a white horse indicates that he is going to be victorious over the powers of evil.

John goes on to say that the one sitting on the white horse is "faithful and true" (Revelation 19:11). God does not lie. He is faithful and true to his covenant and promises. God has penetrating insight into all the matters of man. He is merciful and he is a righteous judge. Often, with our limited knowledge and understanding we may doubt God, but he is faithful and true. There is not a shred of inconsistency with God. He made a way of salvation for mankind and made it clear that anyone who sins is already condemned (John 3:18). To see Jesus Christ on a white horse will be terrifying for those who ignored his love, but for those who accepted him as Lord and Savior, he is faithful and true.

In Revelation 6:8, Death is personified. He's riding a pale horse, which shows that death does not have victory. Paul the apostle wrote, *"O death, where is your victory? O death, where is your sting? The sting of death is sin, and the power of sin is the law; but thanks be to God who gives us the victory through our Lord Jesus Christ"* (I Corinthians 15:55-57, NASB).

Friend, remember Jesus' words: *". . . God so loved the world, that he gave his only begotten Son, that whoever believes in Him shall not perish, but have eternal life"* (John 3:16, NASB). Jesus has won the victory, and some day (and it won't be long), all will see fully just who he is. He is faithful and true, and he will come riding on a white horse.

JESUS WEARING A KINGLY CROWN

John also saw Jesus wearing a kingly crown. It was just a few years earlier when John saw Jesus crucified with a crown of thorns. Imagine what it was like to see Jesus now with many crowns. The imagery here shows that Jesus is king over all aspects of life. We may say that someone "wears many hats." Jesus is the final authority over all areas of existence.

Presently, some authorities ignore the sovereignty of God, but there is a coming day when the King of Kings will wear many crowns. In arrogance, mankind has often set itself up as authority while Jesus Christ wears a diadem. This Greek word means "a crown of royalty." In the Greek culture where the Olympics originated, a person could win a *stephanos*, an achievement crown. Today we hand out medals or present trophies, but Jesus Christ is seen here as wearing a diadem. He is sovereign. He has perfect knowledge and perfect love, and in the final days of time he will judge in righteousness.

The apostle Paul wrote,

A Contrasting Picture of Jesus

*Being found in appearance as a man, He humbled Himself by be-
coming obedient to the point of death, even death on a cross. For this
reason also, God highly exalted Him, and bestowed on Him the name
which is above every name, so that at the name of Jesus every knee will
bow, of those who are in heaven and on earth and under the earth, and
that every tongue will confess that Jesus Christ is Lord, to the glory
of God the Father.*

—Philippians 2:8-11, NASB)

At the end of the 19th century, two French writers went to
visit the well-known French scientist, Pierre Berthelot. Berthelot
was a kind of scientific prophet. He forecasted some of the weap-
ons of mass destruction which would appear in the next century.
He said to the writers, "We have only begun to list the alphabet of
destruction." Silence fell over the meeting. Then the elder of the two
writers said quietly, "I think before that time comes, God will come
like a great gatekeeper with his keys dangling at his waist and say,
'Gentlemen, it's closing time.'"[17]

JESUS WEARING A SPECIAL ROBE

When John saw Jesus at the cross, he was naked, having been stripped
of his robe while he was beaten and crucified. In Revelation, he sees
Jesus wearing a very special robe. It's a robe that has been dipped
or sprinkled in blood. This has two meanings. It identifies him as

17 Source Unknown

Jesus Christ, whose blood was shed, and equally the splattered blood refers to the enemies that he has come to vanquish.

A conversation seems to be happening in Isaiah 63:1-6 (NASB). Person #1: *"Who is this who comes from Edom, with garments of glowing colors from Bozrah, this One who is majestic in His apparel, marching in the greatness of His strength?"* Person #2: *"It is I who speak in righteousness, mighty to save."* Person #1: *"Why is Your apparel red and your garments like the one who treads in the wine press?"* Person #2: *"I have trodden the wine trough alone, and from the peoples there was no man with Me. I also trod them in my anger and trampled them in My wrath; and their lifeblood is sprinkled on My garments."* Wow! What a scene!

God is great in patience and gives all of humanity countless opportunities to know him, but much of mankind has believed Satan's lies and is bent on destruction by their own choices. Psalm 2 is a powerful prophetic Psalm. David speaks of enemies of God who would try to destroy the creator. It is also a sober warning for creation.

> *Why are the nations in an uproar and the peoples devising a vain thing? The kings of the earth take their stand and the rulers take counsel together against the Lord and against His anointed ... Now therefore, O kings, show discernment; take warning, O judges of the earth. Worship the Lord with reverence and rejoice with trembling. Do homage to the Son, that He not become angry, and you perish in the way, for His wrath may soon be kindled. How blessed are all who take refuge in Him!*
>
> —Psalm 2:1-3, 10-12, NASB

A Contrasting Picture of Jesus

JESUS WITH A SHARP SWORD

In John's vision, the sword comes out of Jesus' mouth. It's not a sword at his side. Five times in Revelation it tells us that the sword will come from his mouth. The Bible attests to the healing, creative power of God's voice on numerous occasions. God spoke and everything was created (Genesis 1). Jesus spoke and people not even in his presence were healed (Matthew 8). People were amazed that he only had to speak and even the winds and the waves obeyed (Matthew 8). But at this moment, the sword coming out of his mouth will bring judgment on those who have chosen to ignore the truth of who he is and loved their sin instead. It is a sharp sword. There will be no hope for a way out at this point. Everything will be exposed, and with the accuracy of a skilled surgeon, this sword will finally deal with all the sinfulness in a wicked world.

The word of God is living and powerful, and sharper than any two-edged sword, piercing even to the division of soul and spirit, and of joints and marrow; it is a discerner of the thoughts and intentions of the heart. And there is no creature hidden from His sight, but all things are naked and open to the eyes of Him to whom we must give account (Hebrew 4:12-13). One thing is a certainty, and that is that every human being will either choose the Lordship of Jesus Christ now or will know the wrath of God in the future. How great is sin in the sight of God? It is so great that Jesus was brutalized to win the freedom of mankind. And how great is the love of God to win our freedom?

JESUS' NAME ANNOUNCED

A name is very important. It has meaning attached to it so that others can know the person better. A name is not only a title but a description. The Son of God has 117 names in scripture including "Word," "Lamb of God," "Daystar" and "Christ."

Actually, in this passage of scripture we read three times about his name. Verse 12 says *"He has a name written on Him which no one knows except Himself."* This could mean that no one can fully understand just who Jesus Christ is. After all, he created all things and is like no one else. Verse 13 says *"His name is called The Word of God."* In the gospel of John we read that *"in the beginning was the Word, and the Word was with God, and the Word was God"* (John 1:1, NASB). Jesus Christ is God speaking to humanity. He is God's text message to us. Verse 16 says he has a name written that means *"King of Kings and Lord of Lords."* We also read earlier that his nickname is *"faithful and true"* (verse 11).

Names are important. Jacob literally means "leg puller," or what we would today call a deceiver, but God changed this man and his name became "Israel," meaning a prince who struggled with God. In Matthew, we read that Joseph was told in a dream to name the special baby "Jesus," which is Greek for Joshua, meaning "God will save" (Matthew 1:21). The importance of his name being understood in Revelation 19 is so that all will know just who this is that appears. It's vital for everyone to know who God is, because Satan has lied about his identity. So today I declare that God is good. He saves. He heals. He loves and is greater beyond our wildest imaginations. Nothing compares to the creator.

C. S. Lewis has written these significant words:

God is going to invade this earth in force. But what's the good of saying you're on his side then, when you see the whole natural universe melting away like a dream and something else, something it never entered your head to conceive comes crashing in. Something so beautiful to us and so terrible to others that none of us will have any choice left. This time it will be God without disguise; something so overwhelming that it will strike either irresistible love, or irresistible horror into every creature. It will be too late then to choose your side. There is no use saying you choose to lie down, when it's become impossible to stand up. That will not be the time for choosing; it will be the time when we discover which side we really have chosen, whether we realize it or not.[18]

Now, today, in this moment, is our chance to choose the right side. God is holding back his final judgement to give us that chance. It will not last forever; we must take it or leave it.

One thing is certain: God has made his intentions plain. He created and desires relationship with his creation. Sin is such a horrible thing because of who God is. He is beyond words but some day, all will literally see the Son of God riding on a white horse, wearing a crown, in a special robe and with a sharp sword coming from his mouth. All will know who he is because he has revealed himself by his name—Jesus Christ, the Risen Savior of mankind.

---

18 C.S. Lewis, *The Case for Christianity* (Simon & Schuster, 1989).

Conclusion

If in fact it is true, if in fact Jesus rose from the dead and he is now the coming King who will vanquish his enemies, why would anyone want to choose to be his enemy? And why would anyone choose not to accept his gift of love? Logically, we all would worship him, as those who saw him risen did. The problem we face is that 2000 years of lies have clouded our view of him. Additionally, sin has veiled our eyes. God will unveil our eyes when we humbly admit our sin and give ourselves to him. God raised Jesus from the dead to live for ever, and someday we will see Jesus in the flesh as the disciples did.

When Peter and John went into the tomb of Jesus, they found the cloth that he was buried in. The cloth that was wrapped around the body of Jesus was lying apart from the veil that covered the head of Jesus. Many have contemplated why the head wrap was not with the rest of the burial cloth. No one can know for sure, but I would like to believe that the veil over the dead face of Jesus is analogous to the veil of death that covers our heads before God gives us eternal life.

Once we commit our earthly lives to him, God removes the veil of death. Please understand that this is only one man's conjecture.

Nevertheless, the truth is that God is the giver of life. He raised Jesus from the tomb, and he will also raise you if you have given your life to him.

The apostle Paul wrote,

Since you have been raised to new life with Christ, set your sights on the realities of heaven, where Christ sits in the place of honor at God's right hand. Think about the things of heaven, not the things of earth. For you died to this life, and your real life is hidden with Christ in God. And when Christ, who is your life, is revealed to the whole world, you will share in all his glory.

—Colossians 3:1-4, NLT

Friend, it's all about life and death. Easter is not about bunnies and chocolate. It never has been. The truth about the season is that Jesus Christ of Nazareth rose from the dead and changed everything. Resurrection Sunday is the most significant day of the year. It reminds us that God is the giver of life, and we are the ones who benefit.

Rick Manafo wrote,

The resurrection of Christ is the foundation and culmination of the good news. It gives meaning and substance to our faith. It makes forgiveness for sin possible. It removes the sting of death and robs the grave of final victory. Death is our greatest enemy. We can bounce back from almost anything, but not death. The resurrection of Jesus offers hope in that crucial moment of death.[19]

No matter what life has been for you, understand that the risen Christ gives you and me hope and purpose. God is not our enemy, death is—and Jesus defeated it, not only for himself but for you too.

God makes the invitation for eternal fellowship to all of humanity. If you have read this book but cannot say that you know God personally, I invite you to pray this prayer.

"God, I confess that I am a sinner. Forgive me and make me new. Walk with me and talk with me. Help me to live for you. Surround me with people that will point me back to you. Thank you for saving me and giving me new life. Help me to share what you have done for me and in me."

If you prayed that prayer and meant it, I can say with certainty that you will know and experience the Creator in ways you cannot imagine. If you don't have a Bible, get one and begin to mine the rich jewels that are found in it. Begin with the New Testament book, the Gospel of John. Finally, find others who also know the Creator. You will be amazed by what you learn about him, and then you will naturally tell others about him as your life reflects the discovery of who

---

19 Rick Manafo, "The Resurrection Changes Everything," *inContext Magazine* (2014), http://ca.rzim.org/regional-blog/the-resurrection-changes-everything/.

Appendix I: Why?

Jesus asked more than three hundred questions that are recorded in scripture. One of them is a question that many of us ask ourselves: "Why?" One of the most perplexing verses in scripture is Matthew 27:46, which says, *"...about the ninth hour Jesus cried out with a loud voice, saying, 'Eli, Eli, lema sabachthani?' that is, 'My God, my God, why have you forsaken me?'"* As the Son of God, Jesus knew the plan—so why did he ask "why?" Earlier, he had even announced that he would suffer: *"The Son of man* [his title] *must suffer many things, and be rejected of the elders and chief priests and scribes, and be slain, and be raised the third day"* (Luke 9:22, KJV). Did Jesus forget this, or was he overwhelmed by the pain? Why? He didn't say, "Why did John Telman forsake me," "Why did Peter forsake me" or "Why did Judas forsake me." He said, "My God."

Some have concluded that Jesus became sin and God turned his back on him. Numerous popular songs have been written that lead us to think this way, but it could not be further from the truth. Jesus Christ was not abandoned by God, and in appendix 2 we will show that he did not become sin either.

When Jesus made this powerful statement, he was quoting Psalm 22:1. Have you ever felt far from God when trouble crashes down on you? In numerous psalms, David cried out in pain. Psalms like the 22nd demonstrate a raw honesty. David expresses pain and suffering with deep words of anguish and tears. Those who counsel and comfort others in pain must show that although the pain is real, there is another reality.

Jesus fully felt what it is like to suffer. He felt the pain of being rejected—but did God the Father truly reject him? Could Jesus have been wrong? These are legitimate questions. A greater truth eclipses heart-wrenching pain: when we experience pain, it doesn't mean God has rejected us. Job learned this lesson.

First, God never turns away from the righteous. Secondly, Jesus did not become sin (again, see appendix 2). Suffice it to say, Jesus the pure, holy and righteous Son of God was fully loved by the Father. That love did not change when he was on the cross.

All too often, many have concluded that suffering is a sign of sinfulness. This is patently false. Job's friends believed that he had hidden sin, but God said, *"Have you considered My servant Job? For there is no one like him on the earth, a blameless and upright man, fearing God and turning away from evil"* (Job 1:8, NASB).

After asking "why," Jesus said, *"Father, into your hands I commit my spirit"* (Luke 23:46, NIV). God does not cut and run when we have problems, and he didn't run from Jesus Christ. That is why Jesus entrusted his spirit into the hands of the wise and loving Father God, who was present.

In contrast with Israel, which was unfaithful and consistently sinful, Jesus Christ was the sinless lamb of God.

...you were not redeemed with perishable things like silver or gold from your futile way of life inherited from your forefathers, but with precious blood, as of a lamb unblemished and spotless, the blood of Christ. For He was foreknown before the foundation of the world, but has appeared in these last times for the sake of you who through Him are believers in God, who raised Him from the dead and gave Him glory, so that your faith and hope are in God.

—I Peter I:18-21, NASB

Peter announced that the suffering of Jesus was not because of sin, but because of the opposite. Jesus could suffer and be our perfect sacrifice because he was sinless.

Pain often elicits the question, "Why?" A profound lesson we can learn through this three-letter word is that, like Job, we don't understand the reasons for our suffering, and thus our faith must be in the one who does know all. A "why" seems to drip with more emotion than a "what," "where," "who," "when," or "how."

It's important to note that the chief priests were standing at the cross, mocking Jesus with a psalm: *"He trusted on the Lord that he would deliver him: let him deliver him, seeing he delighted in him"* (Psalm 22:8, KJV). What they did not realize was that the Father *did* delight in the Son (Matt. 3:17). Their conclusion was that he must be an evil man to suffer so. Sadly, our songs have frequently taught the same thing—but Jesus was the pure sinless sin offering for all of humanity. He cried out "Why?" and then trusted in Father God, who had not forsaken him.

APPENDIX II: DID JESUS BECOME SIN?

The apostle Paul wrote, *"...God made Christ, who never sinned, to be the offering for our sin, so that we could be made right with God through Christ"* (2 Corinthians 5:21, NLT). Unfortunately, some versions have incorrectly translated this passage.

A sin offering was, according to the Mosaic Law, a sacrifice to atone for sin. The offering itself was not sinful, but paid the debt of sinfulness through its death. A blemished sacrifice could not be offered.

The word we translate sin is *hamartia* but it is also commonly translated "sin offering" in the Greek version of the Old Testament (Septuagint). The apostle Paul, a student of scripture who wrote the letter to the Corinthians, knew this. It is obvious from the context that Paul was referring to Jesus as a sin offering. In just three chapters alone (Leviticus 4, 5, and 6), *hamartia* is used over twenty times to refer to a sin offering. The New Living Translation picks this up, as seen in the verse quoted above.

The apostle Paul also calls Jesus Christ the "Passover lamb" (1 Corinthians 5:7, NLT). Again, the Passover lamb had to be an unblemished sacrifice (Exodus 12:5). We cannot minimize how important it is to recognize that Jesus was unblemished. He was the one and only perfect sacrifice that could atone for sins of all of humanity. Did Jesus become sin? The simple answer is no—and he could not. He was the perfect, sinless, unblemished sin offering. This fact should cause us to worship him and be deeply grateful.

Isaiah the prophet made it clear. The Messiah, the perfect sinless Son of God (Jesus Christ), *"was pierced for our rebellion"* (Isaiah 53:5, NLT). Further,

> *He had done no wrong and had never deceived anyone. But he was buried like a criminal; he was put in a rich man's grave. But it was the Lord's good plan to crush him and cause him grief. Yet when his life is made an offering for sin, he will have many descendants. He will enjoy a long life, and the Lord's good plan will prosper in his hands.*
> —Isaiah 53:9–10, NLT

Some may wonder if Jesus somehow mystically became sin. This cannot be supported by scripture. What scripture makes clear is that the sin of humanity was laid on him precisely because he did *not* become sin.

Suggested Reading

Anderson, J. Norman. *The Evidence for the Resurrection.* Intervarsity Press, 1950.

Carson, D.A. *Scandalous: The Cross and Resurrection of Jesus.* Crossway, 2010.

Craig, William Lane. *The Son Rises: The Historical Evidence for the Resurrection of Jesus.* Wipf & Stock, 2000.

Craig, William Lane. *New Testament Evidence for the Historicity of the Resurrection of Jesus.* Edwin Mellen, 1989.

Gooding, David, and John Lennox. *Key Bible Concepts.* Myrtlefield House, 2013.

Habermas, Gary R., and Michael R. Licona. *The Case for the Resurrection of Jesus.* Kregel, 2008.

Koukl, Gregory. *The Story of Reality: How the World Began, How It Ends, and Everything Important that Happens in Between.* Zondervan, 2017.

LaHaye, Tim. *Jesus: Who is He?* Multnomah, 1997.

Lewis, C.S. *The Case for Christianity.* Simon & Schuster, 1989.

Lewis, C.S. *Mere Christianity.* HarperSanFrancisco, 2015.

Licona, Michael R. *The Resurrection of Jesus: A New Historiographical Approach.* IVP Academic, 2010.

McDowell, Josh, and Sean McDowell. *Evidence for the Resurrection: What It Means for Your Relationship with God.* Regal, 2008.

Morison, Frank. *Who Moved the Stone?* Zondervan, 1987.

Strobel, Lee. *The Case for Christ: A Journalist's Personal Investigation of the Evidence for Jesus.* Zondervan, 2013.

Strobel, Lee. *The Case for Easter: A Journalist Investigates the Evidence for the Resurrection.* Zondervan, 2014.

Strobel, Lee. *The Case for Faith: A Journalist Investigates the Toughest Objections to Christianity.* Zondervan, 2014.

Strobel, Lee. *The Case for the Resurrection: A First-Century Investigative Reporter Probes History's Pivotal Event.* Zondervan, 2010.

Wright, N.T. *The Resurrection of the Son of God.* Fortress Press, 2016.

Zacharias, Ravi. *Beyond Opinion: Living the Faith We Defend.* Nashville: Thomas Nelson, 2010.

Other books by John W. Telman

Christmas comes around every December, followed by the celebration of a New Year. We recycle the same songs. We cook and eat turkey. But what *is* Christmas? To answer that question, we would be wise to turn to the one who brought the event into being.

The one who is the subject of this book actually walked the dusty roads of the Middle East. Since his birth, he has impacted lives like no other. He has had more followers than anyone in history. He has been hated by many, and misunderstood by countless more, yet his teaching powerfully influences even the lives of those who don't know him. His name is Jesus.

ISBN: 978-1-4866-1322-9
Retail Price: $12.99

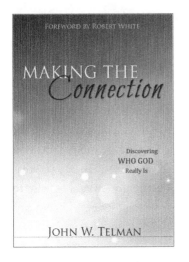

FOREWORD BY ROBERT WHITE

MAKING THE
Connection

Discovering
WHO GOD
Really Is

JOHN W. TELMAN

It is a sad fact that most people who do not believe in God have either an incomplete or false understanding of who the Almighty God is. This book, while valuable for such people, is not intended to be an apologetic, nor a defence. Simply, between the covers of this book is one man's observations of God, who has made himself known.

It's more than eternal life that is at stake. It's fellowship with God. Life without the creator is empty; plastic and worthless. It has no meaning. Fellowship with God is more than knowing facts about God. It is life based on who God is. When anyone has relationship with God, they truly live.

ISBN: 978-1-4866-0488-3
Retail Price: $12.99